Nova Latina

Book 1

R C Bass

Nova Latina Book 1

First published: 2021

This printing: August 2022
ISBN 979 8 5991905 3 0

Also available via Amazon:
Nova Latina Book 1 Specimen Answers ISBN 979 8 7228054 2 3
Streamlined Greek ISBN 978 0 9576725 8 1
Streamlined Greek Answer Book ISBN 978 0 9576725 9 8
Prep School Greek: A workbook leading to CE Level 1 ISBN 978 0 9576725 7 4
More Prep School Greek: A workbook leading to CE Level 2 ISBN 978 1 5272261 3 5
Latin as an Honour Book 1 ISBN 978 0 9576725 0 5
Latin as an Honour Book 2 ISBN 978 0 9576725 3 6
Latin as an Honour Book 3 ISBN 978 0 9576725 4 3
Latin as an Honour Answer Book ISBN 978 0 9576725 5 0
Prep School Latin Book 1 ISBN 978 1 0897232 2 6
Prep School Latin Book 2 ISBN 978 1 6871152 0 1
Prep School Latin Book 3 ISBN 978 1 6871929 2 9
Prep School Latin Book 4 ISBN 978 1 6887813 1 3
Prep School Latin: A Handbook for Students and Teachers ISBN 978 0 9576725 6 7

Published by Galore Park:
Latin Vocabulary for Key Stage 3 ISBN 978 0 9036276 6 5
Latin Pocket Notes ISBN 978 1 9070477 1 8

Typeset by R C Bass

Colbae in memoriam

Contents

Introduction to the Teacher

This volume is an Aldi rather than a Waitrose production: inexpensive and cheerful, with no frills, but hopefully functional. It is a self-contained package providing everything needed to get pupils through all the components of the new CE Level 1 exam. There is an abundance of listings and reference material at the back of the book.

The impetus for writing *Nova Latina* was ISEB's 2019 review of all its syllabuses and examinations, followed by the 2020 consultation period and subsequent publication of its revised specifications, the teaching of which is anticipated to start in September 2021 and whose first summer exam will be in 2023. ISEB's aim was to obviate the need for excessive cramming by reducing subject content whilst not dumbing down, and thereby to ensure that what is known is known well: 'less is more.' On the Latin front, my colleagues Dr Steven Kennedy of Harrow, Nicholas Richards of Christ Church Cathedral School, Oxford, and in particular Ed Clarke of Highfield School, Liphook, were instrumental in this process.

There are two innovations in this current offering. Firstly, it is in what I would call 'quasi-workbook' format: selected exercises can be copied and given to pupils to complete, either electronically or in hard copy, though this selection is of course not prescriptive. My thinking is that to do this for every exercise would be to render the book too unwieldy. Secondly, the vocabulary boxes appear as both Latin-English and English-Latin listings. The premise of my *Latin as an Honour* series was teaching beginners to work from English into Latin from the outset, and I hope that since this approach has found favour with some colleagues they will feel able to use *Nova Latina* in the same way. In the English-Latin listings items marked with an exclamation mark are those prescribed for the sentences set in Question 4 of the paper, and should therefore be accorded priority when it comes to learning vocabulary by heart.

I am very grateful to Nicholas Richards and some of his pupils for trialling these materials in the classroom, and for their helpful and perceptive feedback, both general and particular. The current offering is much less bad as a result; meanwhile constructive feedback of any kind would be most welcome.

A pdf of this volume is available free of charge and on request via email. Colleagues should feel free to circulate these to their pupils, preferably within their own establishment only, and perhaps buy at least a single hard copy! A slim volume of specimen answers is also available.

I am hoping that companion volumes for Level 2, Level 3 and Common Academic Scholarship will follow.

R C Bass
April 2021
robertcharlesbass@gmail.com
www.rcbass.co.uk

Chapter 1
What is Latin?

Latin was the language spoken by the ancient Romans. The city of Rome was situated in the area of central Italy called Latium, which is where Latin gets its name from. Latium is preserved in the name of the region around Rome, Lazio — with, of course, its famous football team.

Rome started off as a small settlement on the banks of the River Tiber. It gradually became more powerful by conquering surrounding areas, then all of Italy, then countries beyond Italy. The area ruled by Rome, which is about the same size as modern Europe and northern Africa, was called the Roman Empire.

When the Romans travelled abroad they took their language with them. The Latin spoken by people in different parts of the Roman Empire gradually altered over hundreds of years, to become modern languages like French, Italian, Spanish and Portuguese. These languages, based on the language of the Romans, are called Romance languages.

Why learn Latin?
'It makes you good at everything else.'
— quote from Emily Wright, a Year 8 student when asked why she was continuing with Latin as an option.

Latin was the main subject taught in this country for more than 500 years. These days not so many are fortunate enough to learn Latin, but it remains a valuable subject for study. It is taught in 70% of independent schools, and not taught in 83% of state schools. You may not think so, but you are privileged to be learning it. Latin is certainly not an easy language to learn, and is not spoken as a modern language any more, so why do we learn it? Well, there are lots of reasons. They may not sound convincing individually, but when taken all together I can assure you that there's no other language quite like it, and certainly not as useful.

Firstly, it's fun. And eventually, if you continue with it at your next school, you will find the whole range of Latin literature, including some superb poetry, accessible to you. This is the essential reason for learning Latin – to be able to read what the Romans wrote. Along the way you will gain all sorts of incidental benefits.

It will equip you, as no other subject at school these days will equip you, with the language of language. You will learn the mechanics of language, how it operates, and be able to apply this to any language you decide to learn later in life – and not just those languages based on Latin. In other words, it will equip you with a sound knowledge of grammar, and of grammatical terms.

Many English words and phrases that we use come from Latin. From the very beginning you will be able to spot connections between Latin words and English words, and you will find that your spelling and understanding of English will improve as you do more Latin. If you study other languages you will be able to spot these connections also. There are some examples on the next page.

Whilst doing all this, you will acquire accuracy and discrimination in your use of words.

English	Latin	French	Italian	Spanish
four	quattuor	quatre	quattro	cuatro
to sing	cantare	chanter	cantare	cantar
to say	dicere	dire	dire	decir
wine	vinum	vin	vino	vino
father	pater	père	padre	padre
good	bonus	bon	buono	bueno
wall	murus	mur	muro	muro
island	insula	île	isola	isla
eagle	aquila	aigle	aquila	águila
dark	obscurus	obscur	oscuro	obscuro

The Latin language is the key which, apart from all the above, will also, of course, open a window in to the thoughts and ideas of the ancient Romans, who had such a widespread influence upon so many aspects of the modern western world.

These, then, are a few of the reasons why we learn Latin. You will begin to appreciate these as we go along. A word of warning, though. As I said earlier, Latin is not an easy language to learn. It demands logical thinking and application. But if you work hard, you will find it rewarding. Anyway, what's the point of being good at something that's easy?

Verbs, persons and number
Verbs are doing words – they describe actions. Here are some examples in English: I am crying. He is smiling. We run. You work. They play.

In Latin, and in other languages you may learn, verbs are set out in groups of six words, each one indicating who is doing the action. These are called the persons.

The first three persons are singular in number – there is only one person doing the action in each case.

The second three persons are plural in number – more than one person is doing the action in each case. The table below will make things clearer:

Person	Number	Person doing the action	English example	In Latin, these parts of the verb will end in:
1st	singular	I	I love *or* I am loving	**-o** *or* **-m**
2nd	singular	You (one person)	You love *or* You are loving (sg)	**-s**
3rd	singular	He or She or It	He/She/It loves *or* He/She/It is loving	**-t**
1st	plural	We	We love *or* We are loving	**-mus**
2nd	plural	You (more than one person)	You love *or* You are loving (pl)	**-tis**
3rd	plural	They	They love *or* They are loving	**-nt**

Chapter 2
Verbs in Latin: the present tense of amo (= I like)

Study this table of the present tense of 'I like' in Latin. 'Tense' here means the time when the action happens, so 'present tense' means that the action is happening now, in the present.

Latin	English
am**o**	I love *or* I am loving
am**as**	You love *or* You are loving *(sg)*
am**at**	He/She/It loves *or* He/She/It is loving
am**amus**	We love *or* We are loving
am**atis**	You love *or* You are loving *(pl)*
am**ant**	They love *or* They are loving

As you will see, in Latin, the front bit ('stem') of the verb indicates what the action is, and the ending (printed in bold) indicates who is doing it.

Lots of Latin verbs end in -o. To translate a simple verb into Latin all you have to do is follow three simple instructions:
1. Find the Latin verb in a dictionary, or word list, or in this book.
2. Remove the -o from the end.
3. Add on the correct personal endings, as summarised in the table below:

Latin personal ending	English person doing the action
-o	I
-as	You (singular – one person)
-at	He/She/It
-amus	We
-atis	You (plural – more than one person)
-ant	They

Conjugations

A conjugation is a family of verbs which behave in the same way. Several verbs follow the pattern of amo, and they are referred to as 'first conjugation verbs'. A few of these are given in the vocabulary box below. Practise reciting the six possible variations, in order, for each verb, and try committing them to memory. This is called 'conjugating a verb'.

Vocabulary Box 1a	
ambulo	I walk
amo	I love *or* I like
canto	I sing
clamo	I shout
habito	I live
specto	I look at *or* I watch

Vocabulary Box 1b	
I live	habito
! I look at *or* I watch	specto
! I love *or* I like	amo
! I shout	clamo
I sing	canto
I walk	ambulo

Exclamation marks in the Vocabulary Box b-listings indicate items liable to occur in the English-into-Latin sentences set in Question 4 of the CE paper, and should therefore be given high priority when it comes to learning vocabulary by heart!

Exercise 2.1

Translate into Latin.
Note: (sg) means singular, and (pl) means plural.
Your Latin sentences do NOT have to start with a capital letter.

1. He likes. ....

2. They walk. ....

3. You (sg) sing. ....

4. He is shouting. ....

5. He lives. ....

6. You (pl) watch. ....

7. We are looking at. ....

8. They shout. ....

9. We walk. ....

10. They love. ....

Handy Help

I live	habito	**-o**	I
I look at, watch	specto	**-as**	You (singular – one person)
I love, like	amo	**-at**	He/She/It
I shout	clamo	**-amus**	We
I sing	canto	**-atis**	You (plural – more than one person)
I walk	ambulo	**-ant**	They

1. Find the verb.
2. Knock off the -o.
3. Add the correct ending.

Exercise 2.2

Translate into Latin.
Note: (sg) means singular, and (pl) means plural.
Your Latin sentences do NOT have to start with a capital letter.

1. We are watching.   ....

2. She is singing.   ....

3. I am watching.   ....

4. They sing.   ....

5. We are shouting.   ....

6. They live.   ....

7. He walks.   ....

8. They watch.   ....

9. She is loving.   ....

10. They look at.   ....

Handy Help

I live	habito		-o	I
I look at, watch	specto		-as	You (singular – one person)
I love, like	amo	1. Find the verb.	-at	He/She/It
I shout	clamo	2. Knock off the -o.	-amus	We
I sing	canto	3. Add the correct ending.	-atis	You (plural – more than one person)
I walk	ambulo		-ant	They

Exercise 2.3

Translate into Latin:

1. We like.
2. I am walking.
3. You (sg) sing.
4. You (sg) are walking.
5. You (pl) live.
6. We sing.
7. She is watching.
8. I shout.
9. You (pl) like.
10. We live.

Exercise 2.4

Translate into Latin:

1. He watches.
2. I love.
3. You (sg) live.
4. We walk.
5. You (pl) sing.
6. They shout.
7. I am singing.
8. They look at.
9. He lives.
10. They walk.

Exercise 2.5

Translate into Latin:

1. He shouts.
2. They live.
3. We watch.
4. You (sg) love.
5. I watch.
6. You (pl) shout.
7. They like.
8. You (sg) shout.
9. I live.
10. You (pl) walk.

The next exercises are your first in working from Latin into English. Remember there are two ways of translating Latin present tenses into English:

1. Using what's called the 'simple present'.
   Example: cantat. *He sings.*

2. Using an -ing word (this is called the 'present continuous').
   Example: cantat. *He is singing.*

Think about what sounds best and try to vary your translations!

Exercise 2.6

Translate into English:

1. habitas.
2. cantatis.
3. amo.
4. spectat.
5. ambulatis.
6. clamant.
7. habitat.
8. amas.
9. clamat.
10. spectant.

Exercise 2.7

Translate into English:

1. ambulas.
2. amant.
3. clamatis.
4. canto.
5. habitant.
6. ambulamus.
7. spectas.
8. ambulo.
9. amamus.
10. cantat.

Exercise 2.8

Translate into English:

1. spectas.
2. ambulant.
3. habitat.
4. clamo.
5. spectatis.
6. cantamus.
7. ambulat.
8. habitatis.
9. spectamus.
10. clamas.

Chapter 3
Nouns in Latin

The noun is the name of a person, place or thing. Lots of Latin nouns end in -a.

Vocabulary Box 2a	
agricola	farmer
domina	mistress
femina	woman
filia	daughter
nauta	sailor
puella	girl
regina	queen

Vocabulary Box 2b		
	daughter	filia
	farmer	agricola
!	girl	puella
	mistress	domina
!	queen	regina
!	sailor	nauta
!	woman	femina

When a noun in doing an action, the verb must have a *he/she/it* ending: **-at**.

Examples:

The farmer is shouting.	agricola clam**at**.
A woman is singing.	femina cant**at**.

(Note: There is no word in Latin for the English words *a*, *an* or *the*)

Exercise 3.1

Translate into Latin.
Your answer will consist of two Latin words.

1. The girl is watching. ....

2. The queen loves. ....

3. The sailor is shouting. ....

4. The daughter is singing. ....

5. A farmer is living. ....

Handy Help

I live	habito
I look at, watch	specto
I love, I like	amo
I shout	clamo
I sing	canto
I walk	ambulo

Exercise 3.2

Translate into Latin.
Your answer will consist of two Latin words.

1. The woman is walking. ....

2. The mistress shouts. ....

3. A sailor is singing. ....

4. The queen watches. ....

5. The daughter is walking. ....

Handy Help

Nouns		Verbs	
daughter	filia	I live	habito
farmer	agricola	I look at, watch	specto
girl	puella	I love, I like	amo
mistress	domina	I shout	clamo
queen	regina	I sing	canto
sailor	nauta	I walk	ambulo
woman	femina		

Verb endings

-o	I
-as	You *(singular: one person)*
-at	He/She/It
-amus	We
-atis	You *(plural: more than one person)*
-ant	They

Exercise 3.3

Translate into Latin:

1. The farmer is shouting.
2. The girl is singing.
3. The mistress is watching.
4. The farmer is walking.
5. The sailor is walking.
6. The daughter loves.
7. The woman shouts.
8. The girl is walking.
9. The queen shouts.
10. The farmer sings.

Exercise 3.4

Translate into English:

1. domina clamat.
2. regina habitat.
3. puella cantat.
4. domina cantat.
5. filia spectat.
6. agricola amat.
7. nauta ambulat.
8. femina clamat.
9. puella spectat.
10. regina ambulat.

Plural nouns

Plural means more than one. In English most (not all!) plural nouns are formed by adding the letter s to the singular.

Examples: dog   plural: dogs
cat   plural: cats

In Latin, the nouns we have met, which end in -a, form their plurals by replacing the -a with -ae. Study the following table:

singular		plural	
Latin	**English**	**Latin**	**English**
agricola	farmer	agricolae	farmers
femina	woman	feminae	women
filia	daughter	filiae	daughters
nauta	sailor	nautae	sailors
puella	girl	puellae	girls
regina	queen	reginae	queens

dy seen, when a **singular** noun is doing an action, the verb must have a *he/she/it*

ples:

The farmer is shouting.   agricola clam**at.**
A woman is singing.   femina cant**at.**

When **plural** nouns are doing an action, the verb must have a *they* ending: -ant.

Examples:

The farmers are shouting. agricolae clam**ant.**
The women are singing.   feminae cant**ant.**

Vocabulary Box 3a	
Nouns	
ancilla	maidservant, slave-girl
dea	goddess
incola	inhabitant
Verbs	
festino	I hurry
intro	I enter, I go in
laboro	I work
navigo	I sail
pugno	I fight

Vocabulary Box 3b	
Nouns	
goddess	dea
inhabitant	incola
! maidservant, slave-girl	ancilla
Verbs	
! I enter, I go in	intro
I fight	pugno
I hurry	festino
I sail	navigo
I work	laboro

Exercise 3.5

Translate into English:

1. incola clamat.

2. incolae clamant.

3. dea cantat.

4. deae cantant.

5. ancillae laborant.

6. ancilla laborat.

7. nautae pugnant.

8. nauta pugnat.

9. ancilla navigat.

10. ancillae navigant.

Exercise 3.6

Translate into English:

1. dea clamat.

2. deae clamant.

3. nautae navigant.

4. nauta navigat.

5. domina clamat.

6. deae spectant.

7. puellae festinant.

8. agricola intrat.

9. filiae cantant.

10. regina ambulat.

Exercise 3.7

Translate into Latin:

1. The goddess is singing.

   ....

2. The goddesses are singing.

   ....

3. The queen enters.

   ....

4. The queens are entering.

   ....

5. Sailors fight.

   ....

6. The maidservant is watching.

   ....

7. The farmers are hurrying.

   ....

8. The inhabitants are working.

   ....

9. The sailor is sailing.

   ....

10. Mistresses shout.

    ....

Handy Help

Nouns		Verbs	
daughter	filia	I enter, go in	intro
farmer	agricola	I fight	pugno
girl	puella	I hurry	festino
goddess	dea	I like	amo
inhabitant	incola	I live	habito
maidservant	ancilla	I look at	specto
mistress	domina	I love	amo
queen	regina	I sail	navigo
sailor	nauta	I shout	clamo
woman	femina	I sing	canto
		I walk	ambulo
		I watch	specto
		I work	laboro

Exercise 3.8

Translate into Latin:

1. The daughter is shouting.
2. The sailors are fighting.
3. The inhabitants are singing.
4. The girl is fighting.
5. The maidservant is working.
6. The women are hurrying.
7. The girl is entering.
8. The farmers are watching.
9. The queen is walking.
10. The mistresses are sailing.

Exercise 3.9

Translate into Latin:

1. The mistress is shouting.
2. The girls are looking.
3. The farmer is working.
4. The goddess sings.
5. The daughters hurry.
6. Queens shout.
7. Sailors sail.
8. The woman is working.
9. The goddesses are fighting.
10. The inhabitant is entering.

Exercise 3.10

Translate into Latin:

1. Goddesses shout.
2. Farmers fight.
3. The daughter is singing.
4. The inhabitants are fighting.
5. Slave girls work.
6. The girls are sailing.
7. The mistress sings.
8. Women fight.
9. The woman is shouting.
10. The inhabitant is working.

Exercise 3.11

Translate into Latin:

1. The sailors are walking.
2. The farmer is shouting.
3. The goddess watches.
4. Girls work.
5. The goddesses hurry.
6. The girl is hurrying.
7. The woman goes in.
8. The sailor is fighting.
9. The mistress is watching.
10. The farmers sing.

Chapter 4
Talking about verbs: Person and Number

Person and *number* are grammatical terms used to identify a particular part of the verb. Here is the table of *amo* you have already met, with the persons and numbers added.

Present tense, first conjugation – amo			
Person	**Number**	**Latin**	**English**
1st	singular	am**o**	I love *or* I am loving
2nd	singular	am**as**	You love *or* You are loving *(sg)*
3rd	singular	am**at**	He/She/It loves *or* He/She/It is loving
1st	plural	am**amus**	We love *or* We are loving
2nd	plural	am**atis**	You love *or* You are loving *(pl)*
3rd	plural	am**ant**	They love *or* They are loving

Person
This is a grammatical term which simply refers to the subject of the verb – in other words, the person doing the action.
- The 1st person singular is the grammatical way of saying *I* am doing something.
- The 2nd person singular refers to *you* (one person only) doing something.
- The 3rd person singular refers to *he* or *she* or *it* doing something.
- The 1st person plural refers to *we* doing something.
- The 2nd person plural refers to *you* (more than one person) doing something.
- The 3rd person plural refers to *they* doing something.

Number
This indicates whether one person (*singular*) or more than one person (*plural*) is doing an action.

Examples
The first person plural of *specto* is *spectamus*, which means *we watch*.
The third person singular of *canto* is *cantat*, which means *he sings*.

navigas (meaning *you sail*) is the second person singular of *navigo*.
habitatis (meaning *you live*) is the second person plural of *habito*.

Exercise 4.1

Give the correct form of the Latin verb, then translate it into English.
The first one is done for you.

1. The 3rd person plural of *canto*. *cantant. They sing.*

2. The 3rd person singular of *habito*. ....

3. The 2nd person singular of *habito*. ....

4. The 2nd person singular of *festino*. ....

5. The 1st person plural of *ambulo*. ....

6. The 3rd person plural of *porto*. ....

7. The 2nd person singular of *navigo*. ....

8. The 2nd person plural of *intro*. ....

9. The 3rd person singular of *clamo*. ....

10. The 3rd person plural of *amo*. ....

11. The 1st person plural of *canto*. ....

Handy Help

Present tense, first conjugation – amo				Verbs	
1st	singular	am**o**	I love *or* I am loving	ambulo	I walk
				amo	I love, like
2nd	singular	am**as**	You love *or* You are loving *(sg)*	canto	I sing
				clamo	I shout
3rd	singular	am**at**	He/She/It loves *or* He/She/It is loving	festino	I hurry
				habito	I live
1st	plural	am**amus**	We love *or* We are loving	intro	I enter, go in
				laboro	I work
2nd	plural	am**atis**	You love *or* You are loving *(pl)*	laudo	I praise
				navigo	I sail
3rd	plural	am**ant**	They love *or* They are loving	paro	I prepare
				pugno	I fight
				specto	I look at, watch

Exercise 4.2

Translate the Latin verb, then gives its person and number. The first one is done for you.

1. laboratis.   *You work. 2nd person plural.*

2. cantas.   ....

3. clamant.   ....

4. pugnamus.   ....

5. intrat.   ....

6. habitat.   ....

7. amant.   ....

8. festinatis.   ....

9. portas   ....

10. ambulat.   ....

11. spectamus.   ....

Handy Help

Present tense, first conjugation – amo				Verbs	
1st	singular	am**o**	I love *or* I am loving	ambulo	I walk
				amo	I love, like
2nd	singular	am**as**	You love *or* You are loving *(sg)*	canto	I sing
				clamo	I shout
3rd	singular	am**at**	He/She/It loves *or* He/She/It is loving	festino	I hurry
				habito	I live
1st	plural	am**amus**	We love *or* We are loving	intro	I enter, go in
				laboro	I work
2nd	plural	am**atis**	You love *or* You are loving *(pl)*	laudo	I praise
				navigo	I sail
3rd	plural	am**ant**	They love *or* They are loving	paro	I prepare
				pugno	I fight
				specto	I look at, watch

Chapter 5
Subjects, objects and Latin word order

Things are going well so far, aren't they? You are more or less working from left to right in both English and Latin. That is about to change, because Latin word order is usually not the same as English word order. This will become clear when we look at the next grammatical topic, subjects and objects. But before dealing with these in Latin, it will be necessary to explain what these terms mean in English first.

It's quite simple:

The subject of a verb is the person doing the action – the doer.

The object of a verb is the person or thing on the receiving end of the action – the receiver. So, in a sentence like:

Tom chases Jerry.

Tom is the subject of the verb – he is the one doing the chasing. Jerry is the object of the verb – he is the one being chased.

The Latin nouns we have met so far end in -a in the singular.

Example: *puella spectat.* The girl is watching.

In this sentence, *puella* is the subject of the verb – she is doing the watching.

But what happens when someone is watching her? In other words, when she becomes the object of the verb, or the receiver of the action? How would you say, in Latin, He is watching the girl. ?

What happens is this. To show that the noun, ending in -a, is not the subject (doer) but the object (receiver) of the verb, its ending changes from -a to -am. In other words, you stick the letter m on the end.

So:
puellam spectat. He is looking at the girl.

Similarly:
aquam portamus. We are carrying water.

and:
reginam amo. I like the queen.

Note that the Latin verb – unlike English – stays at the end of the sentence. This is where you will usually find the verb in a Latin sentence – at the end.

Beware – Latin word order is usually not the same as English word order!

Quick Summary
  Latin singular subjects (doers) end in **-a.**
  Latin singular objects (receivers) end in **-am.**
  Latin verbs (doing words) usually come **at the end of a sentence.**

Vocabulary Box 4a	
Nouns	
aqua	water
cena	dinner, meal
hasta	spear
pecunia	money
silva	wood, forest
Verbs	
aedifico	I build
laudo	I praise
neco	I kill
paro	I prepare
voco	I call

Vocabulary Box 4b		
Nouns		
!	dinner, meal	cena
!	money	pecunia
!	spear	hasta
	water	aqua
	wood, forest	silva
Verbs		
!	I build	aedifico
!	I call	voco
!	I kill	neco
!	I praise	laudo
!	I prepare	paro

Exercise 5.1

Translate into Latin. Your answer will consist of two Latin words only.
Note: (sg) means singular, and (pl) means plural.
Your Latin sentences do NOT have to start with a capital letter.

1. We are building a villa. ....

2. They praise the queen. ....

3. She is preparing dinner. ....

4. I like money. ....

5. You (pl) are entering the wood. ....

6. He is looking at the water. ....

7. We kill the mistress. ....

8. You (sg) are preparing a spear. ....

9. She is calling the maidservant. ....

10. I am praising the goddess. ....

Exercise 5.2

Translate into Latin:

1. I am looking at the villa.
2. We like the queen.
3. They are entering the villa.
4. We are calling ther sailor.
5. He kills the woman.
6. You (sg) are calling the maidservant.
7. She is preparing a meal.
8. They praise the farmer.
9. You (pl) are building a villa.
10. He likes the spear.

Exercise 5.3

Translate into English:

1. pecuniam amat.
2. aquam intro.
3. deam laudas.
4. cenam amamus.
5. villam intrat.
6. dominam vocatis.
7. reginam necant.
8. silvam intras.
9. ancillam vocant.
10. nautam spectamus.

Exercise 5.4

Translate into Latin:

1. The girl is singing.

....

2. We like the girl.

....

3. The mistress is calling.

....

4. We praise the mistress.

....

5. The maidservant is shouting.

....

6. You (sg) are calling the maidservant.

....

7. They are looking at the money.

....

8. We are preparing dinner.

....

9. The daughter is working.

....

10. You (pl) are entering the villa.

....

Exercise 5.5

Translate into English:

1. domina vocat. ....

2. dominae vocant. ....

3. dominam amamus. ....

4. nautae navigant. ....

5. nautam laudas. ....

6. regina cantat. ....

7. ancillae laborant. ....

8. ancillam vocant. ....

9. cenam paras. ....

10. feminae clamant. ....

Handy Help

Nouns		Verbs	
ancilla	maidservant	amo	I like
cena	dinner, meal	canto	I sing
domina	mistress	clamo	I shout
femina	woman	laboro	I work
nauta	sailor	laudo	I praise
regina	queen	navigo	I sail
		paro	I prepare
		voco	I call

Chapter 6 Subject, Object, Verb

We have now come across three kinds of noun endings:

-a This indicates a single subject (doer of an action):
Example: puella clamat. *The girl is shouting.*

-ae This indicates a plural subject (doers of an action):
Example: puellae clamant. *The girls are shouting.*

-am This indicates a singular object (receiver of an action):
Example: puellam amat. *He likes the girl.*

Sometimes a sentence will contain a named subject (doer) as well as an object (receiver). In this case the usual Latin word order is:

subject (-a/-ae endings) + object (-am ending) + verb at the end

Examples: nauta puellam amat.   *The sailor (he) likes the girl.*
nautae puellam amant.   *The sailors (they) like the girl.*

Vocabulary Box 5a	
Nouns	
insula	island; block of flats
patria	country, homeland
poeta	poet
sagitta	arrow
turba	crowd
via	road, street, way
Verbs	
oppugno	I attack
porto	I carry
rogo	I ask, ask for
supero	I overcome, overpower

Vocabulary Box 5b	
Nouns	
arrow	sagitta
country, homeland	patria
crowd	turba
island; block of flats	insula
poet	poeta
! road, street, way	via
Verbs	
I ask, ask for	rogo
I attack	oppugno
! I carry	porto
I overcome, overpower	supero

Note on *rogo* (I ask, I ask for)
This verb can be used of asking a person, or asking for **something**, or asking **a person for something**. In each case the person being asked, or the thing being asked for, must have an object/receiver ending (-am). Study these examples:

ancilla dominam rogat.   *The maidservant asks the mistress.*
ancilla pecuniam rogat.   *The maidservant asks for money.*
ancilla dominam pecuniam rogat. *The maidservant asks the mistress for money.**

*This last sentence is an example of what some grammar books refer to as a 'double accusative' construction.

Exercise 6.1

Translate into Latin.

1. The sailors are attacking the island.
   ....

2. The woman is carrying an arrow.
   ....

3. The inhabitants love the country.
   ....

4. The girls are asking for money.
   ....

5. The farmers are building a road.
   ....

6. The mistress overpowers the maidservant.
   ....

7. The crowd is watching the girl.
   ....

8. The poet is asking for water.
   ....

9. The arrows overpower the woman.
   ....

10. The poets are looking at the arrow.
    ....

Handy Help

Nouns				Verbs	
arrow	sagitta	mistress	domina	I ask for	rogo
country	patria	money	pecunia	I attack	oppugno
crowd	turba	poet	poeta	I build	aedifico
farmer	agricola	road	via	I carry	porto
girl	puella	sailor	nauta	I look at	specto
inhabitant	incola	water	aqua	I love	amo
island	insula	woman	femina	I overpower	supero
maidservant	ancilla			I watch	specto

21

Exercise 6.2

Translate into English:

1. agricola filiam portat. ....

2. incolae cenam rogant. ....

3. poeta patriam laudat. ....

4. nautae pecuniam amant. ....

5. feminae nautam spectant. ....

6. turba poetam necat. ....

7. incolae reginam laudant. ....

8. nautae aquam amant. ....

9. turba patriam laudat. ....

10. poeta cenam parat. ....

Handy Help

Nouns				Verbs	
agricola	farmer	nauta	sailor	amo	I like, love
aqua	water	patria	homeland	laudo	I praise
cena	dinner, meal	pecunia	money	neco	I kill
femina	woman	poeta	poet	paro	I prepare
filia	daughter	regina	queen	porto	I carry
incola	inhabitant	turba	crowd	rogo	I ask
				specto	I watch, look at

Chapter 7
Plural Objects. The cases.

Plural Objects

If you remember, we have come across three kinds of noun endings:

-**a**   This indicates a single subject (doer of an action):
        Example: puell**a** clamat.   *The girl is shouting.*

-**ae**   This indicates a plural subject (doers of an action):
        Example: puell**ae c**lamant. *The girls are shouting.*

-**am**   This indicates a singular object (receiver of an action):
        Example: puell**am** amat.   *He likes the girl.*

To make this complete, we now need to add the ending for plural objects. This is -**as**. So:

-**as**   This indicates a plural object (receivers of an action):
        Example: puell**as a**mat.   *He likes the girls.*

The cases: nominative and accusative

There are special grammatical terms used to refer to subjects (doers) and objects (receivers).

The word **nominative** is used to refer to a **subject**.
The word **accusative** is used to refer to an **object**.

Words like nominative and accusative are called cases. The case of a Latin noun indicates what job that noun is doing in the sentence.

The four noun endings we have met can be set out as a table, like this:

name of case	job done in sentence	singular	plural
nominative	subject (doer)	puell**a**	puell**ae**
accusative	object (receiver)	puell**am**	puell**as**

As you may be coming to realise by now, word endings are vitally important in Latin!

Exercise 7.1

Translate into English:

1. ancillas vocatis.
2. poetam laudamus.
3. incolae clamant.
4. silvas intratis.
5. aquam rogat.
6. vias aedificat.
7. poeta laborat.
8. turbam spectamus.
9. hastas parant.
10. ancillam specto.

Exercise 7.2

Translate into Latin.

1. The girl likes the poet.   ....

2. The girl likes poets.   ....

3. The girls like the poet.   ....

4. Girls like poets.   ....

5. The mistress watches the slave girl.   ....

6. The mistress watches the slave girls.   ....

7. The mistresses watch the slave girls.   ....

8. The mistresses watch the slave girl.   ....

9. The queen praises the inhabitants.   ....

10. The sailors are preparing arrows.   ....

Handy Help

Nouns				Verbs	
arrow	sagitta	queen	regina	I like	amo
girl	puella	sailor	nauta	I praise	laudo
mistress	domina	slave girl	ancilla	I prepare	paro
poet	poeta			I watch	specto

name of case	job done in sentence	singular	plural
nominative	subject (doer)	puella	puellae
accusative	object (receiver)	puellam	puellas

24

Exercise 7.3

Translate into English:

1. agricola ancillam amat.

   ....

2. agricola ancillas amat.

   ....

3. agricolae ancillam amant.

   ....

4. agricolae ancillas amant.

   ....

5. filia silvam intrat.

   ....

6. incolae vias aedificant.

   ....

7. poeta deas laudat.

   ....

8. nautae hastas portant.

   ....

9. domina ancillas vocat.

   ....

10. ancillae dominam spectant.

   ....

name of case	job done in sentence	singular	plural
nominative	subject (doer)	puell**a**	puell**ae**
accusative	object (receiver)	puell**am**	puell**as**

Handy Help

aedifico	I build	filia	daughter	poeta	poet
agricola	farmer	hasta	spear	porto	I carry
amo	I love	incola	inhabitant	silva	wood
ancilla	maidservant	intro	I enter	specto	I look at
dea	goddess	laudo	I praise	via	road
domina	mistress	nauta	sailor	voco	I call

Chapter 8
Adverbs and Conjunctions

Adverbs are words which describe verbs. They tell us when, where or how something happens.

<table>
<tr><td colspan="2">Vocabulary Box 6a</td></tr>
<tr><td colspan="2">Adverbs</td></tr>
<tr><td>bene</td><td>well</td></tr>
<tr><td>diu</td><td>for a long time</td></tr>
<tr><td>non</td><td>not</td></tr>
<tr><td>numquam</td><td>never</td></tr>
<tr><td>saepe</td><td>often</td></tr>
<tr><td>semper</td><td>always</td></tr>
<tr><td colspan="2">Conjunctions</td></tr>
<tr><td>et</td><td>and</td></tr>
<tr><td>sed</td><td>but</td></tr>
<tr><td colspan="2">Nouns</td></tr>
<tr><td>epistula</td><td>letter</td></tr>
<tr><td>ira</td><td>anger</td></tr>
<tr><td>terra</td><td>land, earth</td></tr>
<tr><td>unda</td><td>wave</td></tr>
<tr><td>villa</td><td>wave</td></tr>
</table>

<table>
<tr><td colspan="3">Vocabulary Box 6b</td></tr>
<tr><td colspan="3">Adverbs</td></tr>
<tr><td>!</td><td>always</td><td>semper</td></tr>
<tr><td></td><td>for a long time</td><td>diu</td></tr>
<tr><td></td><td>never</td><td>numquam</td></tr>
<tr><td>!</td><td>not</td><td>non</td></tr>
<tr><td>!</td><td>often</td><td>saepe</td></tr>
<tr><td></td><td>well</td><td>bene</td></tr>
<tr><td colspan="3">Conjunctions</td></tr>
<tr><td>!</td><td>and</td><td>et</td></tr>
<tr><td></td><td>but</td><td>sed</td></tr>
<tr><td colspan="3">Nouns</td></tr>
<tr><td></td><td>anger</td><td>ira</td></tr>
<tr><td></td><td>land, earth</td><td>terra</td></tr>
<tr><td>!</td><td>letter</td><td>epistula</td></tr>
<tr><td>!</td><td>villa, house</td><td>villa</td></tr>
<tr><td></td><td>wave</td><td>unda</td></tr>
</table>

Position: these adverbs go just before the main verb at the end of a sentence, **in the same order as they occur in English.**

Study these examples:

The sailor works.	nauta laborat.
The sailor does **not** work.	nauta **non** laborat.
The sailor works **well**.	nauta **bene** laborat.
The sailor does **not** work **well**.	nauta **non bene** laborat.
The sailor does **not often** work **well**.	nauta **non saepe bene** laborat.

Conjunctions

As you probably know from English already, conjunctions are joining words. The two most common conjunctions in Latin are *et* (and) and *sed* (but). Like adverbs, they do not have different endings, and in a Latin sentence you will find them where you would expect to!

Study these examples:

The sailor **and** the farmer (they) are working.	nauta **et** agricola laborant.
I am singing **but** (I am) working.	canto **sed** laboro.
The girl is singing **but** (she is) not working.	puella cantat **sed** non laborat.

Exercise 8.1

Translate into Latin.

1. You (sg) often hurry.

   ....

2. We always work well.

   ....

3. Farmers often fight.

   ....

4. He never works for a long time.

   ....

5. Girls always sing well.

   ....

6. The farmer always works well.

   ....

7. Maidservants often hurry.

   ....

8. Sailors sing well.

   ....

9. Sailors never sing well.

   ....

10. The poet does not always work well.

   ....

Handy Help

Adverbs		Nouns		Verbs	
always	semper	farmer	agricola	I fight	pugno
for a long time	diu	girl	puella	I hurry	festino
never	numquam	maidservant	ancilla	I sing	canto
not	non	poet	poeta	I work	laboro
often	saepe	sailor	nauta		
well	bene				

Chapter 9
Families of verbs. *moneo*.

A conjugation is a family of verbs which behave in the same way. All the verbs we have met so far behave like *amo*, I like. This group of verbs, or conjugation, is called the **first conjugation**. In dictionaries and wordlists verbs which behave like *amo* will have a number in brackets after it, to show that it belongs to the first conjugation, like this:

navigo (1) I sail

It is now time to meet a second family of verbs – the **second conjugation**. These verbs behave in a slightly different way from those which go like *amo*. Study the table below:

Present tense, second conjugation – moneo			
Person	*Number*	*Latin*	*English*
1st	singular	mon**eo**	I warn *or* I am warning
2nd	singular	mon**es**	You warn *or* You are warning *(sg)*
3rd	singular	mon**et**	He/She/It warns *or* He/She/It is warning
1st	plural	mon**emus**	We warn *or* We are warning
2nd	plural	mon**etis**	You warn *or* You are warning *(pl)*
3rd	plural	mon**ent**	They warn *or* They are warning

As you can see, the letter *e* between the stem and ending is a distinctive feature of this conjugation. Remember to pronounce the Latin letter *e* like the *e* in b<u>e</u>t.

It is easy to spot verbs which belong to the second conjugation: the first person singulars (the I form of the verb) all end in *-eo*.

Here are some new verbs. They all go like *moneo*, second conjugation, so a (2) appears after them. Practise chanting them through, following the pattern of *moneo*. Reciting a verb in this way is called (if you remember from page 3!) **conjugating** it.

Vocabulary Box 7a	
deleo (2)	I destroy
habeo (2)	I have
moneo (2)	I warn
moveo (2)	I move
teneo (2)	I hold
terreo (2)	I frighten
timeo (2)	I fear
video (2)	I see

Vocabulary Box 7b		
!	I destroy	deleo (2)
!	I fear	timeo (2)
	I frighten	terreo (2)
!	I have	habeo (2)
	I hold	teneo (2)
	I move	moveo (2)
!	I see	video (2)
!	I warn	moneo (2)

Practising Second Conjugation Verbs

Exercise 9.1

Translate into English:

1. monemus.
2. habet.
3. terres.
4. tenent.
5. videt.
6. deletis.
7. movent.
8. terreo.
9. timemus.
10. tenemus.

Exercise 9.2

Translate into English:

1. tenet.
2. vides.
3. timeo.
4. habent.
5. videtis.
6. mones.
7. monet.
8. terretis.
9. movemus.
10. delent.

Exercise 9.3

Translate into English:

1. nautae non timent.
2. pecuniam moves.
3. sagittae delent.
4. puella timet.
5. nautam moneo.
6. hastas movemus.
7. puellas terremus.
8. filiam habeo.
9. hastas tenent.
10. villam videtis.

Exercise 9.4

Translate into English:

1. puellae timent.
2. ancilla dominam timet.
3. regina incolas monet.
4. turba puellam terret.
5. nautae insulam delent.
6. agricola hastam tenet.
7. feminae nautas timent.
8. aqua nautam non terret.
9. domina filiam habet.
10. poeta epistulam delet.

Exercise 9.5

Translate into Latin:

1. They fear.
2. We have.
3. You (sg) see.
4. He holds.
5. We destroy.
6. They warn.
7. You (pl) frighten.
8. I fear
9. We move.
10. He sees.

Exercise 9.6

Translate into Latin:

1. The girl is afraid.
2. I see the island.
3. We are holding spears.
4. He is moving the money.
5. They have daughters.
6. You (sg) fear sailors.
7. We see the letter.
8. It holds water.
9. He warns the inhabitants.
10. You (pl) see the queen.

Chapter 10
Consolidation

Exercise 10.1

Give the correct form of the verb, then translate your answer into English:

1. The 1st person plural of *amo*.
2. The 2nd person singular of *moneo*.
3. The 3rd person singular of *laboro*.
4. The 3rd person plural of *timeo*.
5. The 2nd person plural of *festino*.
6. The 2nd person singular of *oppugno*.
7. The 1st person singular of *deleo*.
8. The 1st person plural of *habito*.
9. The 3rd person plural of *canto*.
10. The 3rd person singular of *video*.

Exercise 10.2

Translate into Latin:

1. You (pl) destroy.
2. We are holding.
3. They are sailing.
4. You (sg) fear.
5. I am watching.
6. He praises.
7. She has.
8. We see.
9. We overcome.
10. They fight.

Exercise 10.3

Translate into Latin:

1. Arrows destroy.
2. The poet is afraid.
3. Mistresses warn.
4. Farmers fight well.
5. The slave girls see.
6. Queens are not afraid.
7. The sailor never sings.
8. The crowd is working.
9. Sailors often sail.
10. The girl and the woman are hurrying.

Exercise 10.4

Translate into Latin:

1. They have money.
2. We praise the goddess.
3. She is preparing dinner.
4. You (pl) frighten the slave girls.
5. He likes girls.
6. We are asking the queen.
7. I am warning the inhabitants.
8. You (sg) are building a villa.
9. They are looking at the letter.
10. We enter the wood.

Exercise 10.5

Translate into English:

1. regina pecuniam semper habet.

   ....

2. nautae numquam bene laborant.

   ....

3. agricola hastas et sagittas saepe portat.

   ....

4. puellae vias numquam bene aedificant.

   ....

5. domina ancillas non saepe terret.

   ....

Exercise 10.6

Translate into Latin:

1. Girls always fear arrows.

   ....

2. Slave girls never have money.

   ....

3. Poets often fear women.

   ....

4. Sailors never prepare spears well.

   ....

5. The queen often frightens the girls.

   ....

Chapter 11
The irregular verb 'to be'

The verbs we have met so far belong to either the first conjugation (like *amo*) of the second conjugation (like *moneo*).

Some verbs don't follow such regular patterns. These are called 'irregular' verbs, and the most common irregular verb in most languages is the verb *to be*. Here it is in Latin:

Present tense, 'to be' – sum			
Person	*Number*	*Latin*	*English*
1st	singular	**sum**	I am
2nd	singular	**es**	You are (singular)
3rd	singular	**est**	He is/She is/It is
1st	plural	**sumus**	We are
2nd	plural	**estis**	You are (plural)
3rd	plural	**sunt**	They are

Special Rule
The verb *to be* is different from other verbs: it does not take an accusative object. Can you see why? It's like an equals sign. In the sentence *Marcus is a sailor* Marcus is not doing anything **to** the sailor; he **is** a sailor. Marcus = sailor. Think of it as nominative = nominative.

Examples:

He is a sailor.	nauta est. (singular)
They are sailors.	nautae sunt (plural)
The woman is a slave-girl.	femina ancilla est. (singular)
The inhabitants are women.	incolae feminae sunt (plural)

Exercise 11.1

Translate into English:

1. nautae estis.
2. agricola est.
3. dea non est.
4. feminae sunt.
5. regina est.

6. nauta es.
7. regina sum.
8. incolae sumus.
9. epistula est.
10. sagittae sunt

Exercise 11.2

Translate into Latin:

1. She is a slave-girl.

....

2. We are farmers.

....

3. You are a poet.

....

4. You are sailors.

....

5. We are women.

....

6. It is a villa.

....

7. They are spears.

....

8. You are not a slave-girl.

....

9. He is a sailor.

....

10. We are not farmers.

....

Exercise 11.3

Translate into Latin:

1. The sailor is a poet.

....

2. The woman is the queen.

....

3. The queen is not a slave-girl.

....

4. A slave-girl is not often a queen.

....

5. The inhabitants are often farmers.

....

Chapter 12
The genitive case: 'of'

The case of a noun, if you remember, indicates what job that noun is doing in a Latin sentence. We have met two cases so far, the nominative (subject or doer) case and the accusative (object or receiver case). Here is a reminder of their endings:

name of case	job done in sentence	singular	plural
nominative	subject (doer)	puella	puellae
accusative	object (receiver)	puellam	puellas

We are now going to meet a third case. It is called the **genitive** case. The genitive case is the 'of' or 'of the' case – it indicates the owner of something.

The genitive singular ending is **-ae**. So 'of the girl' is puellae.
The gentivie plural ending is **-arum**. So 'of the girls' is puellarum.

A genitive word will usually follow another noun, this first noun indicating what is being possessed. Study the following examples, paying attention to the endings of the nouns.

Examples:

The money of the poet.	pecunia poetae.
The money of the poets.	pecunia poetarum.
The daughter of the sailor.	filia nautae.
The daughters of the sailor.	filiae nautae.
A crowd of girls.	turba puellarum.
Crowds of girls.	turbae puellarum.
I like the daughter of the farmer.	filiam agricolae amo.

Here is an updated noun table showing all the endings of *puella*-type nouns we have met:

name of case	job done in sentence	singular	plural
nominative	subject (doer)	puella	puellae
accusative	object (receiver)	puellam	puellas
genitive	*of the*	puellae	puellarum

You will have spotted that the genitive singular ending is the same as the nominative plural ending. Don't panic! Just remember, your first word will have a nominative ending to indicate what is being possessed; your second word will have a genitive ending to indicate the possessor.

The English Apostrophe

The English apostrophe replaces the word *of*, and causes all sorts of problems, but it's quite simple: the apostrophe goes immediately after the possessor. So:

The money of the farmer	=	The **farmer's** money.
The money of the farmers	=	The **farmers'** money.

Exercise 12.1

Translate into Latin:

1. The money of the queen. ....

2. The money of the queens. ....

3. The daughters of the sailor. ....

4. The daughters of the sailors. ....

5. The inhabitants of the island. ....

6. The crowd of slave girls. ....

7. The spear of the farmer. ....

8. The queen of the island. ....

9. The arrows of the farmers. ....

10. The slave-girl of the poet. ....

Handy Help

name of case	job done in sentence	singular	plural
nominative	subject (doer)	puella	puellae
accusative	object (receiver)	puellam	puellas
genitive	*of the*	puellae	puellarum

Nouns

arrow	sagitta	money	pecunia
crowd	turba	poet	poeta
daughter	filia	queen	regina
farmer	agricola	sailor	nauta
inhabitant	incola	slave-girl	ancilla
island	insula	spear	hasta

Exercise 12.2

Translate into English:

1. The inhabitants of the island always fight well.

   ....

2. The goddess of the island never frightens the inhabitants.

   ....

3. The daughter of the farmer is a slave girl.

   ....

4. Sailors never attack the villa of the queen.

   ....

5. The slave-girls of the poet like the money of the sailors.

   ....

Your first Latin passage

Well done! - you have now reached the stage where you are ready to tackle your first Latin passage rather than just a set of sentences. One of the main points of learning Latin is to be able to read what the Romans wrote about.

As you read more Latin passages you will learn all sorts of useful hints and ways in which to translate sentences so that they sound like decent English.

The layout will be new to you. Here are three things you will notice:

1. The passage will always have a title, to help you understand what's going on. Read the title carefully – it will give you clues about the meaning of some words, and may help you with some English spellings.

2. The lines of Latin are numbered down the left, for easy reference.

3. Some words in the passage are underlined. The meanings of these words, or information about them, are given down the right, in the margin. There is a smart term for these notes in the right-hand margin: they are called 'marginal glosses'.

Right – let's get going.

Exercise 12.3

Translate into English:

The Roman general Julius Caesar decides to attack Britain.

1 Britannia insula est. Britannia <u>magna</u> insula est.

  <u>multi</u> incolae in Britannia habitant. patriam <u>suam</u>

  amant. bene laborant. vias et villas aedificant.

  <u>quod</u> Britanniam amant, <u>laeti</u> sunt.

5 Iulius Caesar <u>Romanus</u> est. incolas Britanniae

  non amat. nautas <u>igitur</u> vocat. nautae sagittas et

  hastas parant, <u>trans</u> aquam navigant et

  Britanniam oppugnant. turbae incolarum, <u>ubi</u>

  <u>Romanos</u> vident, timent.

magna = big

multi = many
suam = their own

quod = because
laeti = happy
Romanus = Roman

igitur = therefore

trans = across

ubi = when
Romanos = Romans
(accusative/object/receiver ending)

(A copy of this passage in workbook format can be found on page 108)

Grammar Check

Here is a checklist of the grammatical terms you have met so far. Hopefully you will already know some of these from English. Make sure you are familiar with them!

accusative	This is the object case, indicating the receiver of an action.
adverbs	These are words which describe verbs and tell you how, when or where something happens. e.g. *bene* (well), *saepe* (often).
case	nominative (subject/doer), accusative (object/receiver), genitive (*of the*).
conjugation	A family of verbs which behave in the same way. e.g. *amo* (1) is in the first conjugation; *moneo* (2) is in the second conjugation.
conjunction	A joining word. e.g. *et* (and), *sed* (but).
genitive	This is the *of the* case, indicating the possessor.
nominative	This is the subject case, indicating the doer of an action.
noun	A person, place or thing.
number	Whether a noun or verb is singular or plural.
object	The receiver of an action.
person	1st person singular = I; 2nd person singular = You; 3rd person singular = He, She, It; 1st person plural = We; 2nd person plural = You; 3rd person plural = They.
plural	More than one of something.
singular	One of something.
subject	The doer of an action.
tense	The time when a verb takes place. A tense will be in the past, present or future.
verb	A doing word.

Chapter 13
Nouns: the rest of the cases

As you know, a Latin noun has different endings to show what job the noun is doing in the sentence. The endings we have met so far have been 'person or persons doing' (subject/nominative) endings (*-a/-ae*), 'person or persons done to' (object/accusative) endings (*-am/-as*), and the 'of the' (genitive) endings (*-ae/-arum*). These different endings indicate the noun's **case**. There are six cases in Latin. Here is a table showing which job in a sentence each case indicates. The vocative, dative and ablative cases will be new to you, so study these carefully.

name of case	job	English example in bold
nominative	subject (doer) of verb	The **girl** is working hard.
vocative	person spoken to	**Girl**, what are you doing?
accusative	object (receiver) of verb	The mistress punishes the **girl**.
genitive	*of*	The teacher **of the girl** is clever.
dative	*to, for*	I give money **to the girl**.
ablative	*by, with (= by means of), (away) from*	He attacks the boy **with his spear**.

Recognising the cases

Exercises 13.1, 13.2 and 13.3
If you were translating the sentences in the following three exercises into Latin, into which case would you put each of the underlined words? Use the table above to help.

Exercise 13.1
1. The Queen of <u>Hearts</u> she baked some <u>tarts</u>.
2. The <u>teacher</u> bribed the children with a <u>Mars Bar</u>.
3. <u>We</u> travelled by <u>taxi</u>.
4. <u>Girl</u>, why are you running from the <u>room</u>?
5. Will <u>you</u> do a favour for <u>me</u>?

Exercise 13.2
1. The <u>teacher</u> is chasing the <u>boy</u>.
2. He shouts, '<u>Boy</u>, what are <u>you</u> doing?'
3. The teacher beats the <u>boy</u> with a <u>stick</u>.
4. 'Why are you beating me, <u>sir</u>?' asks the <u>boy</u>.
5. The <u>master</u> replies to the <u>boy</u>, 'Silence, boy!'

Exercise 13.3
1. I always work for my <u>teachers</u>.
2. <u>Work</u> irritates me.
3. The fields were covered with <u>mist</u>.
4. <u>Boy</u>, why are you smoking a <u>cigarette</u>?
5. With the <u>help</u> of the <u>public</u> the <u>police</u> returned the <u>dog</u> to its <u>owner</u>.

Here are all the cases of *puella*. It is worth chanting them through and learning them by heart!

Singular		
nominative	subject (doer)	puell**a**
vocative	person spoken to	puell**a**
accusative	object (receiver)	puell**am**
genitive	*of*	puell**ae**
dative	*to, for*	puell**ae**
ablative	*by, with, from*	puell**a**
Plural		
nominative	subjects (doers)	puell**ae**
vocative	persons spoken to	puell**ae**
accusative	objects (receivers)	puell**as**
genitive	*of*	puell**arum**
dative	*to, for*	puell**is**
ablative	*by, with, from*	puell**is**

Vocabulary Box 8a		**Vocabulary Box 8b**	
ira	anger	anger	ira
terra	land, earth	land, earth	terra
unda	wave	wave	unda
Graecia	Greece	Greece	Graecia
Roma	Rome	Rome	Roma
Troia	Troy	Troy	Troia

(The words in the box above complete all the puella-*type nouns you need to know for Common Entrance Level 1.)*

As you know, a family of **verbs** which behave in the same way is called a **conjugation**. A family of **nouns** which behave in the same way is called a **declension**.

This is a good point to explain some of the conventions of displaying Latin nouns in wordlists and dictionaries.

For example: *regina, -ae f. queen*

The first word is the nominative singular.
The second word is the genitive singular (<u>not</u> the plural!).
The dash (-) before the genitive is a short cut to save space, and indicates that the stem (front bit) of the noun must be assumed. So, *regina, -ae* is short for *regina, reginae*.

Gender
Latin nouns have a grammatical gender, like *le* and *la* words in French. Most nouns ending in *-a* are feminine in gender, but a handful (*agricola, incola, poeta, nauta*) are masculine.

m. is short for masculine, and f. is short for feminine.

These conventions are followed in the listings of all the Level 1 nouns on the next page.

Summary of *puella*-type (first declension) nouns
Latin–English

agricola, -ae m.	farmer		patria, -ae f.	country, homeland
ancilla, -ae f.	maidservant, slave-girl		pecunia, -ae f.	money
aqua, -ae f.	water		poeta, -ae m.	poet
cena, -ae f.	dinner, meal		puella, -ae f.	girl
dea, -ae f.	goddess		regina, -ae f.	queen
domina, -ae f.	mistress		Roma, -ae f.	Rome
epistula, -ae f.	letter		sagitta, -ae f.	arrow
femina, -ae f.	woman		silva, -ae f.	wood, forest
filia, -ae f.	daughter		terra, -ae f.	land, earth
Graecia, -ae f.	Greece		Troia, -ae f.	Troy
hasta, -ae f.	spear		turba, -ae f.	crowd
incola, -ae m.	inhabitant		unda, -ae f.	wave
ira, -ae f.	anger		via, -ae f.	road, street
nauta, -ae m.	sailor		villa, -ae f.	villa

Summary of *puella*-type (first declension) nouns
English–Latin

anger	ira, -ae f.		meal	cena, -ae f.
arrow	sagitta, -ae f.		mistress	domina, -ae f.
country	patria, -ae f.		money	pecunia, -ae f.
crowd	turba, -ae f.		poet	poeta, -ae m.
daughter	filia, -ae f.		queen	regina, -ae f.
dinner	cena, -ae f.		road	via, -ae f.
earth	terra, -ae f.		Rome	Roma, -ae f.
farmer	agricola, -ae m.		sailor	nauta, -ae m.
forest	silva, -ae f.		slave-girl	ancilla, -ae f.
girl	puella, -ae f.		spear	hasta, -ae f.
goddess	dea, -ae f.		street	via, -ae f.
Greece	Graecia, -ae f.		Troy	Troia, -ae f.
homeland	patria, -ae f.		villa	villa, -ae f.
inhabitant	incola, -ae m.		water	aqua, -ae f.
land	terra, -ae f.		wave	unda, -ae f.
letter	epistula, -ae f.		woman	femina, -ae f.
maidservant	ancilla, -ae f.		wood	silva, -ae f.

Exercise 13.4

Translate into Latin (your answer must be a single Latin word):

1. by letters
2. with anger
3. of the villa
4. by water
5. for money
6. by land
7. for the inhabitants
8. to the sailors
9. girls! (being spoken to)
10. for dinner

Exercise 13.5

Translate into Latin (your answer must be a single Latin word):

1. for the daughter ....
2. by road ....
3. from the islands ....
4. with arrows ....
5. of the mistress ....

6. for women ....
7. to slave-girls ....
8. by letter ....
9. for the queen ....
10. to the queens ....

Exercise 13.6

Translate into Latin (your answer must be two words long):

1. for the mistress of the slave-girls ....

2. to the queen of Greece ....

3. with the arrows of the inhabitants ....

4. by the anger of the goddess ....

5. with the letter of the poet ....

6. for the daughter of the woman ....

7. for the dinner of the farmer ....

8. with the money of the queen ....

9. to the inhabitants of the homeland ....

10. with crowds of girls ....

Chapter 14
Practising nouns like puella

Vocabulary Box 9a	
cur?	why?
do (1)	I give
fortiter	bravely
frustra	in vain
magnopere	greatly, very much
quod	because
respondeo (2)	I reply, answer
statim	immediately

Vocabulary Box 9b	
because	quod
bravely	fortiter
greatly, very much	magnopere
immediately	statim
in vain	frustra
I give	do (1)
I reply, answer	respondeo (2)
why?	cur?

Exercise 14.1

Translate into English:

1. domina, cur non semper bene laboras?

....

2. domina pecuniam ancillae dat.

....

3. cur nautas timetis, puellae?

....

4. nautas timemus quod nautas non amamus.

....

5. turba nautarum incolas insulae hastis oppugnat.

....

Exercise 14.2

Translate into English:

1. nautae Troiam statim oppugnant.

....

2. femina filiam rogat, sed filia non respondet.

....

3. agricolae puellas hastis terrent.

....

4. nauta viam incolis aedificat.

....

5. nautae hastas incolis terrae dant.

....

The words on this page marked with an asterisk (*), *her* and *your*, are words indicating possession, and words like these (such as *my, his, our, their*) can often be ignored when translating into Latin when it is obvious who the owner(s) is/are. Similarly, when translating out of Latin it can sometimes be a nice touch to add an appropriate possessive word in English.

For example:

agricola filiam amat = The farmer loves a/the daughter.

= The farmer loves <u>his</u> daughter.

Exercise 14.3

Translate into Latin:

1. The woman is preparing dinner for her* daughter.

   ....

2. I often give water to the inhabitants.

   ....

3. We are preparing a meal for the girls.

   ....

4. The poet gives the letter to the queen immediately.

   ....

5. You are destroying the villas with your* spears, farmers.

   ....

Exercise 14.4

Translate into Latin:

1. The slave-girl does not reply well to the queen.

   ....

2. Sailors, why are you attacking Rome with your* spears?

   ....

3. The mistress never gives money to her* slave-girls.

   ....

4. The inhabitants of Greece always fight bravely.

   ....

5. We are attacking the island with the spears of the sailors.

   ....

Chapter 15
Third and Fourth Conjugation Verbs

We have already met first conjugation verbs like *amo*, and second conjugation verbs like *moneo*. There are two more conjugations – third and fourth. They are quite similar to each other, so we can deal with both of them together.

The third conjugation sample verb is *rego*, meaning 'I rule'.
The fourth conjugation sample verb is *audio*, meaning 'I hear' or 'I listen' or even 'I listen to.'

Compare the following two tables carefully. What are their similarities and differences?

Present tense, third conjugation – rego			
Person	*Number*	*Latin*	*English*
1st	singular	reg**o**	I rule *or* I am ruling
2nd	singular	reg**is**	You rule *or* You are ruling *(sg)*
3rd	singular	reg**it**	He/She/It rules *or* He/She/It is ruling
1st	plural	reg**imus**	We rule *or* We are ruling
2nd	plural	reg**itis**	You rule *or* You are ruling *(pl)*
3rd	plural	reg**unt**	They rule *or* They are ruling

Present tense, fourth conjugation – audio			
Person	*Number*	*Latin*	*English*
1st	singular	aud**io**	I hear *or* I am hearing
2nd	singular	aud**is**	You hear *or* You are hearing *(sg)*
3rd	singular	aud**it**	He/She/It hears *or* He/She/It is hearing
1st	plural	aud**imus**	We hear *or* We are hearing
2nd	plural	aud**itis**	You hear *or* You are hearing *(pl)*
3rd	plural	aud**iunt**	They hear *or* They are hearing

Vocabulary Box 10a	
audio (4)	I hear, listen, listen to
bibo (3)	I drink
curro (3)	I run
discedo (3)	I depart, leave
dormio (4)	I sleep
lego (3)	I read, choose
mitto (3)	I send
rego (3)	I rule
scribo (3)	I write
venio (4)	I come

Vocabulary Box 10b	
I drink	bibo (3)
I depart, leave	discedo (3)
I read, choose	lego (3)
I rule	rego (3)
I run	curro (3)
I send	mitto (3)
I write	scribo (3)
I come	venio (4)
I hear, listen, listen to	audio (4)
I sleep	dormio (4)

Beware of audio!
If you are translating 'listen to' into Latin you must put the object of the verb – what is being listened to – into the **accusative** case. Do not be misled by the 'to' of 'listen to' into putting it into the dative (*to* or *for*) case.

You may find it easier to think of the meaning of *audio* simply as *I hear*.

So: He is listening to the queen = He hears the queen = regin**am** audit.

Exercise 15.1

Translate into English:

1. He rules.

2. You (pl) are sending.

3. They depart.

4. I am coming.

5. We are sleeping.

6. You (sg) are running.

7. They read.

8. She is writing.

9. We are drinking.

10. You (pl) are listening.

Exercise 15.2

Translate into Latin:

1. legis.

2. mittimus.

3. dormit.

4. veniunt.

5. scribis.

6. discedo.

7. bibunt.

8. mittit.

9. scribunt.

10. audio.

Exercise 15.3

Translate into English:

1. nauta bibit.

2. incolae currunt.

3. puella legit.

4. poetae scribunt.

5. agricolae discedunt.

6. reginam audimus.

7. epistulam scribis.

8. aquam bibo.

9. pecuniam mittunt.

10. puellae dormiunt.

Exercise 15.4

Translate into Latin
(your answers must be two words long):

1. The queen rules.

2. The farmers are coming.

3. The inhabitants are sleeping.

4. Sailors drink.

5. You (sg) are reading a letter.

6. He is drinking water.

7. They write letters.

8. We listen to the goddess.

9. He is sending the money.

10. They rule the land.

Exercise 15.5

Translate into English:

1. poetae epistulas non semper bene scribunt.

   ....

2. turba nautarum statim discedit.

   ....

3. nautae aquam non saepe bibunt.

   ....

4. cur epistulam legis, puella?

   ....

5. regina Troiam semper bene regit.

   ....

Exercise 15.6

Translate into Latin:

1. Sailors often fight.

   ....

2. Why are you running, girls?

   ....

3. We are running because we fear the goddess.

   ....

4. The slave girls always listen to the mistress.

   ....

5. The farmers are departing immediately.

   ....

6. The poet loves Rome greatly.

   ....

7. The inhabitants do not always run well.

   ....

8. Why are you always sleeping, slave girl?

   ....

9. Poets are always writing letters.

   ....

10. Women never drink for a long time.

    ....

Present Tense Verb Revision

You have now covered the present tenses of all the regular verb conjugations, as well as the irregular verb *sum* ('I am').

How many of these exercises can you do 'blind' – that is, without looking anything up?

Exercise 15.7

Translate into English:

1. amant.
2. deles.
3. currit.
4. venit.
5. sunt.
6. das.
7. regitis.
8. videt.
9. laboras.
10. necatis

Exercise 15.8

Translate into English:

1. currunt.
2. laudas.
3. sumus.
4. audis.
5. spectatis.
6. respondet.
7. teneo.
8. scribit.
9. portas.
10. timent.

Exercise 15.9

Translate into English:

1. timet.
2. intrat.
3. es.
4. mittimus.
5. voco.
6. legit.
7. scribunt.
8. oppugnant.
9. monemus.
10. bibitis.

Exercise 15.10

Translate into English:

1. videmus.
2. clamo.
3. respondent.
4. estis.
5. dormis.
6. habitat.
7. habet.
8. superant.
9. veniunt.
10. terres.

Exercise 15.11

Translate into English:

1. aedificamus.
2. movetis.
3. discedis.
4. festinas.
5. est.
6. pugnat.
7. sum.
8. rogamus.
9. ambulatis.
10. tenent.

Exercise 15.12

Translate into Latin:

1. He fears.
2. They reply.
3. She gives.
4. They praise.
5. We rule.
6. You (sg) sleep.
7. We write.
8. He is attacking.
9. We are.
10. They depart.

Exercise 15.13

Translate into Latin:

1. They are.   ....
2. He sees.   ....
3. You (sg) shout.   ....
4. They are calling.   ....
5. We reply.   ....
6. He sends.   ....
7. I am writing.   ....
8. We are coming.   ....
9. You (pl) sleep.   ....
10. They are listening.   ....

Exercise 15.14

Translate into Latin:

1. We kill.   ....
2. He asks.   ....
3. We fight.   ....
4. They are sailing.   ....
5. She praises.   ....
6. You (sg) enter.   ....
7. I hurry.   ....
8. You (pl) work.   ....
9. They see.   ....
10. He is.   ....

Exercise 15.15

Translate into Latin:

1. You (sg) are.   ....
2. We are listening.   ....
3. I am running.   ....
4. He is drinking.   ....
5. You (pl) rule.   ....
6. He replies.   ....
7. You (sg) fear.   ....
8. She is preparing.   ....
9. We are praising.   ....
10. They ask.   ....

Exercise 15.16

Translate into Latin:

1. You (pl) are.   ....
2. He is sleeping.   ....
3. We write.   ....
4. They come.   ....
5. I see.   ....
6. You (sg) frighten.   ....
7. We are walking.   ....
8. We live.   ....
9. They are writing.   ....
10. He is working.   ....

Chapter 16
Second declension masculine nouns like *servus*

Not surprisingly, the second family of nouns we are meeting is called the **second declension**. Second declension masculine nouns are easy to spot: they almost all end in *-us*. The model noun we use for this declension is the word for a slave, *servus*.

case	job	singular	plural
nominative	subject (doer)	serv**us**	serv**i**
vocative	person spoken to	serv**e**	serv**i**
accusative	object (receiver)	serv**um**	serv**os**
genitive	*of the*	serv**i**	serv**orum**
dative	*to* or *for*	serv**o**	serv**is**
ablative	*by* or *with* or *from*	serv**o**	serv**is**

Vocabulary Box 11 consists of nouns whose endings are exactly the same as those of *servus*. As usual, you may be able to spot connections between some of these new words and words you already know in English.

Vocabulary Box 11a	
amicus	friend
cibus	food
deus	god
dominus	master
equus	horse
filius	son
gladius	sword
maritus	husband
murus	wall
servus	slave

Vocabulary Box 11b		
	food	cibus
!	friend	amicus
!	god	deus
!	horse	equus
	husband	maritus
!	master	dominus
!	slave	servus
!	son	filius
!	sword	gladius
!	wall	murus

Exercise 16.1

Translate into Latin:

1. of the slave
2. for food
3. friends!
4. to the god
5. for the masters
6. of the horse
7. for (my) son
8. with walls
9. with a sword
10. for (my) husband

Exercise 16.2

Translate into English:

1. equus currit.
2. deos timemus.
3. maritum habeo.
4. gladios parant.
5. amici clamant.
6. cibum non habet.
7. servi dormiunt.
8. murum aedificamus.
9. filius non audit.
10. amici veniunt.

Exercise 16.3

Translate into English:

1. regina maritum non habet.
2. servi muros oppugnant.
3. ancillae amicos non habent.
4. cur deos semper timemus?
5. agricola cibum amat.
6. puellae equos amant.
7. servi dominos saepe timent.
8. filius gladium et hastam tenet.
9. marite, cur filium non amas?
10. murum gladiis oppugnamus.

Exercise 16.4

Translate into English:

1. servi dominos non semper amant.

....

2. servi, cur deos timetis?

....

3. agricolae hastas saepe portant.

....

4. equos reginae spectamus.

....

5. reginae maritos non semper habent.

....

6. puellae cibum equis saepe dant.

....

7. amice, cur cibum servo das?

....

8. turba servorum venit.

....

9. maritus reginae gladium semper portat.

....

10. feminae maritos pecuniam saepe rogant.

....

Exercise 16.5

Translate into Latin:

1. The maidservants fear the master.

....

2. Masters never listen to slaves.

....

3. The slave is preparing food for the horse.

....

4. The master's horse (= the horse of the master) is always drinking water.

....

5. The slaves are attacking the villa with swords.

....

Chapter 17
Reading Practice and Grammar Questions

Exercise 17.1
Translate into English.

Julius Caesar and his Romans attack the Britons.

1 Britanni in ora stant. Romanos spectant. Britanni Romanos non amant et Romani Britannos non amant. Romani, ubi gladios et hastas et equos parant, ad Britannos currunt. clamant. Romani et

5 Britanni fortiter et diu pugnant. Romani multos Britannos gladiis et hastis necant. tandem Britanni, quod fessi sunt, fugiunt. Romani iam laeti sunt. rident. Caesar Romanos laudat quod bene pugnant.

Britannus = a Briton	
ora = shore	
sto = I stand	
Romanus = a Roman	
ubi = when	
ad = towards	
diu = for a long time	
multos = many	
tandem = finally	
fessi = tired	
fugio = I flee	
iam = now	
laeti = happy	
rideo (2) = I laugh	

(A copy of this passage in workbook format can be found on page 109.)

Answering Grammar Questions
One of the skills you will need to master for Common Entrance is how to identify the grammatical terms used to describe the various bits of the language. You should be familiar with many of these already from English. It is a good idea to get used to answering these sorts of questions as soon as possible, so that you are well prepared for your exams at the end of Year 8.

Included in this section of the exam will be a question asking you to work out a connection between an English word and the Latin word it comes from. This is called a **derivation**, and is different from a translation. For example, the English translation of *aqua* is *water* but possible derivations are *aquatic* or *aquarium*.

Exercise 17.2
Answer these questions. They are based on the passage above. Complete English sentences are not required.

1. From the passage, give, in Latin, one example of each of the following:
   a. a first conjugation verb;
   b. a second conjugation verb;
   c. a third conjugation verb;
   d. an adverb.

2. **stant** (line 1). Explain the connection between this word and the English word *stationary.*

3. **spectant** (line 1). Give the person and number of this verb.

4. **Romanos** (line 2). Give the case of this noun.

5. **currunt** (line 4). Give the Latin subject of this verb.

51

Sentences and Subordinate Clauses In English and Latin

A clause is a part of a sentence that contains a verb. Sometimes the clause will actually form a complete sentence.
Example: *The pupils ran away.*

Now look at this sentence:
The pupils, when they saw the teacher approaching, ran away.

The words between the commas here form what is called a **subordinate clause.**
If this subordinate clause were removed, the main sentence (*The pupils ran away*) would still make sense.

The subordinate clause itself (*when they saw the teacher approaching*) does not make sense on its own; it sounds awkward and incomplete.

We have already met, in Exercise 17.1, two kinds of subordinate clauses in Latin: those introduced by *ubi* (= when) and those introduced by *quod* (= because):

Romani, ubi gladios et hastas et equos parant, ad Britannos currunt.
The Romans, **when they prepare their swords and spears and horses,** run towards the Britons.

Caesar Romanos laudat quod bene pugnant.
Caesar praises the Romans **because they fight well**.

Note in each sentence how the subordinate clause, printed in bold, does not make sense on its own, and how the rest of the sentence makes perfect sense if the subordinate clause is removed.

How to translate *ubi*- and *quod*- clauses into natural English
Latin likes to put the subject/doer of the verb at or near the very beginning of the sentence:
Romani, ubi gladios et hastas et equos parant, ad Britannos currunt.
The Romans, **when they prepare their swords and spears and horses**, run towards the Britons.

This does not always make for natural English. If you move the *when* to the beginning of the sentence, the English often sounds better:
So: **When** the Romans prepare their swords and spears and horses, they run towards the Britons.

The same trick can apply to *quod*-clauses:
servi, quod dominus clamat, timent.
Literally this means: The slaves, because their master is shouting, they are afraid.

But moving the *because* to the beginning of the sentence makes the English a lot nicer:
Because their master is shouting, the slaves are afraid.

Another option in English is to postpone the subordinate clause to the end:
The slaves are afraid **because** their master is shouting.

Now try this translation technique yourself by doing Exercise 17.3. Each sentence contains a subordinate clause beginning with either an *ubi* or a *quod*. Concentrate on making your version sound like natural English, not a translation of a piece of Latin!

Vocabulary Box 12a		Vocabulary Box 12b	
iam	now, already	at last, finally	tandem
rideo (2)	I laugh	I laugh	rideo (2)
sto (1)	I stand	now, already	iam
tandem	at last, finally	I stand	sto (1)
ubi	when	when	ubi

Note on *ubi*

When *ubi* starts a clause which does <u>not</u> end in a question mark, translate it as 'when'.
When *ubi* starts a clause which <u>does</u> end in a question mark, translate it as 'where?'
(You will meet this second usage in Chapter 29, page 85 – line 9 of the passage.)

Examples: servus, ubi dominum videt, timet.
***When** the slave sees the master, he is afraid.*

ubi est dominus?
***Where** is the master?*

Exercise 17.3

Translate into English:

1. nautae, ubi oppugnant, clamant.

....

2. poeta, ubi reginam videt, timet.

....

3. incolae, quod nautae oppugnant, timent.

....

4. servi, ubi villam delent, discedunt.

....

5. incolae, quod patriam amant, non discedunt.

....

6. servus, ubi dominus vocat, semper statim venit.

....

7. femina, quod iram reginae timet, discedit.

....

8. ancillae, ubi cibum parant, numquam cantant.

....

9. dominus, ubi servos terret, ridet.

....

10. feminae, ubi turbam nautarum vident, timent.

....

Chapter 18
Prepositions

Prepositions are little words – like *in*, *with*, *towards* – which go just in front of nouns. In other words, they are pre-positioned (geddit?).

In Latin, some prepositions have to be followed with nouns which have accusative endings, and other prepositions have to be followed by nouns which have ablative endings. Which prepositions take which endings will be made clear in wordlists.

In your reading passages we have already come across the following prepositional phrases:

in Britannia	*in Britain*	(in + ablative = in)
trans aquam	*across the water*	(trans + accusative = across)
in ora	*on the shore*	(in + ablative = on)
ad Britannos	*towards the Britons*	(ad + accusative = towards)

Vocabulary Box 13 lists all the Latin prepositions you need to know for Common Entrance Level 1.

Vocabulary Box 13a	
ad + accusative	to, towards
contra + accusative	against
in + accusative	into
per + accusative	through, along
prope + accusative	near
trans + accusative	across
a/ab + ablative	away from, from
cum + ablative	with
de + ablative	down from, about
e/ex + ablative	out of
in + ablative	in, on

Vocabulary Box 13b	
across	trans + accusative
against	contra + accusative
into	in + accusative
near	prope + accusative
through, along	per + accusative
to, towards	ad + accusative
away from, from	a/ab + ablative
down from, about	de + ablative
in, on	in + ablative
out of	e/ex + ablative
with	cum + ablative

Beware of tricky *in*!

Be very careful with the Latin preposition **in**: its meaning depends on the case of the word following it. Look at the following examples:

The girl is standing **on** the wall.	puella **in muro** stat.	(in + abl.)
The girl is running **into** the wall.	puella **in murum** currit.	(in + acc.)

Right. Lots of exercises practising prepositions coming up.

Exercise 18.1

Translate into English:

1. de muro
2. ex villa
3. cum amicis
4. prope viam
5. in epistula

6. contra servos
7. ab insula
8. trans viam
9. in villam
10. ad turbam

a or ab? e or ex?

When translating into Latin use these guidelines:

When the following word starts with a vowel or an h (in other words, a, e, i, o, u or h). use *ab* and *ex*.

away from the islands	ab insulis
out of the water	ex aqua

Otherwise, use either!

away from the villa	a villa or ab villa
out of the country	e patria or ex patria

(In the second instance, put what you like the sound of! In English it is easier to say *an apple* rather than *a apple*, and some people say *an hotel* rather than *a hotel*. Sometimes the Romans themselves were not sure which to put, and even used both options in the same sentence!)

Exercise 18.2

Translate into Latin:

1. on the wall ....   6. near the islands ....

2. in the villa ....   7. against the horses ....

3. into the villa ....   8. along the road ....

4. with friends ....   9. through the woods ....

5. in a letter ....   10. out of the villas ....

Handy Help

across	trans + acc.
against	contra + acc.
into	in + acc.
near	prope + acc.
through, along	per + acc.
to, towards	ad + acc.
away from, from	a/ab + abl.
down from, about	de + abl.
in, on	in + abl.
out of	e/ex + abl.
with	cum + abl.

sg	nominative	puella	servus
	vocative	puella	serve
	accusative	puellam	servum
	genitive	puellae	servi
	dative	puellae	servo
	ablative	puella	servo
pl	nominative	puellae	servi
	vocative	puellae	servi
	accusative	puellas	servos
	genitive	puellarum	servorum
	dative	puellis	servis
	ablative	puellis	servis

Exercise 18.3

Translate into English:

1. in villa bibo.

....

2. ab insula navigamus.

....

3. cur trans viam curris, puella?

....

4. femina ad maritum festinat.

....

5. contra nautas pugnamus.

....

6. nautae in insula dormiunt.

....

7. cur ab insula non disceditis, nautae?

....

8. reginae epistulas ad amicos non saepe scribunt.

....

9. nauta pecuniam ex villa movet.

....

10. agricolae contra nautas saepe pugnant.

....

Handy Help

across	trans + acc.
against	contra + acc.
into	in + acc.
near	prope + acc.
through, along	per + acc.
to, towards	ad + acc.
away from, from	a/ab + abl.
down from, about	de + abl.
in, on	in + abl.
out of	e/ex + abl.
with	cum + abl.

sg			
	nominative	puella	servus
	vocative	puella	serve
	accusative	puellam	servum
	genitive	puellae	servi
	dative	puellae	servo
	ablative	puella	servo
pl	nominative	puellae	servi
	vocative	puellae	servi
	accusative	puellas	servos
	genitive	puellarum	servorum
	dative	puellis	servis
	ablative	puellis	servis

Exercise 18.4

Translate into Latin:

1. The sailors are sailing towards the island.

....

2. The poet is writing a letter in the villa.

....

3. The farmer is building a wall with his friends.

....

4. Mistress, why are you running into the villa?

....

5. The queen sends her son away from the island

....

6. Sailors never run away from waves.

....

7. The inhabitants are building a wall on the island.

....

8. The daughter of the queen often runs across the road.

....

9. The maidservant is preparing dinner in the master's villa.

....

10. The slaves are running out of the woods towards the villa.

....

Handy Help

across	trans + acc.
against	contra + acc.
into	in + acc.
near	prope + acc.
through, along	per + acc.
to, towards	ad + acc.
away from, from	a/ab + abl.
down from, about	de + abl.
in, on	in + abl.
out of	e/ex + abl.
with	cum + abl.

sg	nominative	puella	servus
	vocative	puella	serve
	accusative	puellam	servum
	genitive	puellae	servi
	dative	puellae	servo
	ablative	puella	servo
pl	nominative	puellae	servi
	vocative	puellae	servi
	accusative	puellas	servos
	genitive	puellarum	servorum
	dative	puellis	servis
	ablative	puellis	servis

Chapter 19
Other nouns like *servus*

We have already met second declension nouns which end in *-us* and go like *servus*.
Study the tables of *boy*, *field* and *man* below. They are almost the same as *servus*. What are the differences?

case	job	puella (girl) f.	servus (slave) m.	puer (boy) m.	ager (field) m.	vir (man) m.
first declension			**second declension**			
SINGULAR						
nominative	subject (doer)	puella	servus	puer	ager	vir
vocative	person spoken to	puella	serve	puer	ager	vir
accusative	object (receiver)	puellam	servum	puerum	agrum	virum
genitive	*of the*	puellae	servi	pueri	agri	viri
dative	*to* or *for*	puellae	servo	puero	agro	viro
ablative	*by* or *with* or *from*	puella	servo	puero	agro	viro
PLURAL						
nominative	subjects (doers)	puellae	servi	pueri	agri	viri
vocative	persons spoken to	puellae	servi	pueri	agri	viri
accusative	objects (receivers)	puellas	servos	pueros	agros	viros
genitive	*of the*	puellarum	servorum	puerorum	agrorum	virorum
dative	*to* or *for*	puellis	servis	pueris	agris	viris
ablative	*by* or *with* or *from*	puellis	servis	pueris	agris	viris

Things to note:
- The endings of *puer*, *ager* and *vir* are the same as those of *servus*, except for the nominative and vocative singular.
- *puer* keeps its e all the way through.
- *ager* drops its e from the accusative singular onwards.
- *vir* is a bit of a one-off, but is the same as *servus* except for the nominative and vocative singular.

Vocabulary Box 14a	
ager (drops its e)	field
liber (goes like *ager*)	book
magister (goes like *ager*)	teacher
puer (keeps its e)	boy
vir	man

Vocabulary Box 14b	
! book	liber (goes like *ager*)
! boy	puer (keeps its e)
field	ager (drops its e)
! man	vir
! teacher	magister (goes like *ager*)

Exercise 19.1

Translate into English:

1. vir currit.

   ....

2. viri scribunt.

   ....

3. puer es.

   ....

4. librum legis.

   ....

5. magistrum non amo.

   ....

6. magistri saepe legunt.

   ....

7. puer cantat.

   ....

8. in libris numquam scribo.

   ....

9. magistri pueros et puellas numquam terrent.

   ....

10. domini cibum servis numquam dant.

   ....

Exercise 19.2

Translate into Latin:

1. The master is reading a book.

   ....

2. The boys like the teacher.

   ....

3. Girls always like boys.

   ....

4. The man has a field.

   ....

5. The teacher frightens the man.

   ....

Exercise 19.3

Translate into Latin:

1. The man warns the teacher.

....

2. Farmers often work in fields.

....

3. We are giving a book to the boy.

....

4. The men are standing in the field.

....

5. A crowd of slaves is frightening the boys with swords.

....

Handy Help

		first declension	second declension			
case	job	puella (girl) f.	servus (slave) m.	puer (boy) m.	ager (field) m.	vir (man) m.
SINGULAR						
nominative	subject (doer)	puella	servus	puer	ager	vir
vocative	person spoken to	puella	serve	puer	ager	vir
accusative	object (receiver)	puellam	servum	puerum	agrum	virum
genitive	*of the*	puellae	servi	pueri	agri	viri
dative	*to* or *for*	puellae	servo	puero	agro	viro
ablative	*by* or *with* or *from*	puella	servo	puero	agro	viro
PLURAL						
nominative	subjects (doers)	puellae	servi	pueri	agri	viri
vocative	persons spoken to	puellae	servi	pueri	agri	viri
accusative	objects (receivers)	puellas	servos	pueros	agros	viros
genitive	*of the*	puellarum	servorum	puerorum	agrorum	virorum
dative	*to* or *for*	puellis	servis	pueris	agris	viris
ablative	*by* or *with* or *from*	puellis	servis	pueris	agris	viris

Chapter 20
Romulus and Remus: Part 1

Exercise 20.1
Translate the following passage into good English.

King Amulius decides to take drastic action against Rhea's two little boys, because the god of war is their father.

1 Rhea femina <u>pulchra</u> est. in Italia habitat. <u>duo</u> filios

   habet. filii sunt <u>parvi</u>. <u>pater</u> filiorum est deus Mars. sed

   Rhea non <u>laeta</u> est. non <u>laeta</u> est quod <u>rex</u> patriae,

   Amulius, pueros <u>parvos</u> non amat. Amulius, quod

5 <u>parvos</u> filios Rheae non amat, <u>eos</u> <u>necare</u> <u>constituit</u>.

   <u>nomina</u> puerorum sunt Romulus et Remus.

pulchra = beautiful
duo = two
parvi = small
pater = father
sed = but
laeta = happy
rex = king
parvos = small
eos = them
necare = to kill
constituo (3) = I decide
nomina = names

(A copy of this passage in workbook format can be found on page 110.)

Exercise 20.2

1. From the passage above give, in Latin, an example of:

   a. a second conjugation verb;   ....

   b. a part of the verb 'to be';   ....

   c. a preposition;   ....

   d. an adverb;   ....

   e. a noun in the genitive case.   ....

2. **Italia** (line 1). In which case is this noun?   ....

   Why is this case used? ....

3. **habitat** (line 1). Give the person and number of this verb.

   ....

4. **puerorum** (line 6). Give the case of this noun. ....

Chapter 21
Infinitives: *to*-words

We came across the following sentence in the last reading passage:

Amulius … eos **necare** constituit.
*Amulius decides **to kill** them.*

The words in bold print here are called **infinitives**.
Infinitives are *to*-words; for example, *to run, to laugh, to play*.
In Latin, infinitives usually end in -**re**.

Here is a table of the four conjugations (verb groups) and the irregular verb *to be*, showing their infinitives:

Conjugation	Present	English	Infinitive	English
1st	amo	*I love*	am**are**	*to love*
2nd	moneo	*I warn*	mon**ere**	*to warn*
3rd	rego	*I rule*	reg**ere**	*to rule*
4th	audio	*I hear*	aud**ire**	*to hear*
irregular verb	sum	*I am*	**esse**	*to be*

Position: You will usually find infinitives just before the main verb at the end of a Latin sentence.

They will occur just in front of verbs of preparing (**to** do domething), ordering (someone **to** do something), deciding (**to** do something) and wanting (**to** do something). We've already met the verb *I prepare* – paro (1) – but the other three verbs will be new to you. Here they are:

Vocabulary Box 15a	
constituo (3)	I decide
cupio (3½)*	I want
iubeo (2)	I order

Vocabulary Box 15b	
I decide	constituo (3)
I order	iubeo (2)
I want	cupio (3½)*

* We shall be meeting a handful of 3½ verbs later. They behave like 3rd conjugation (*rego*) verbs in some ways but like 4th conjugation (*audio*) verbs in others. For the moment, just treat *cupio* as an *audio*-type verb.

Examples:

puella **currere** parat.	The girl prepares **to run**.
dominus servum **laborare** iubet.	The master orders the slave **to work**.
vir **pugnare** constituit.	The man decides **to fight**.
puer **scribere** cupit.	The boy wants **to write**.

Exercise 21.1

Translate into English:

1. habitare ....

2. videre ....

3. bibere ....

4. venire ....

5. mittere ....

6. scribere ....

7. tenere ....

8. intrare ....

9. dormire ....

10. laborare ....

Exercise 21.2

Translate into Latin:

1. to look at ....

2. to reply ....

3. to run ....

4. to read ....

5. to fear ....

6. to shout ....

7. to build ....

8. to move ....

9. to lead ....

10. to hurry ....

Handy Help

Conjugation	Present	English	Infinitive	English
1st	amo	*I love*	am**are**	*to love*
2nd	moneo	*I warn*	mon**ere**	*to warn*
3rd	rego	*I rule*	reg**ere**	*to rule*
4th	audio	*I hear*	aud**ire**	*to hear*
irregular verb	sum	*I am*	**esse**	*to be*

Exercise 21.3

Translate into English:

1. cantare paramus. ....

2. clamare cupio. ....

3. scribere amamus. ....

4. dormire cupiunt. ....

5. bibere constituis. ....

Exercise 21.4

Translate into Latin:

1. They order the boys to write.

....

2. I want to be a poet.

....

3. Boys never want to work.

....

4. The poet decides to write a book.

....

5. The slaves are preparing to attack the villa.

....

Handy Help

Conjugation	Present	English	Infinitive	English
1st	amo	*I love*	am**are**	*to love*
2nd	moneo	*I warn*	mon**ere**	*to warn*
3rd	rego	*I rule*	reg**ere**	*to rule*
4th	audio	*I hear*	aud**ire**	*to hear*
irregular verb	sum	*I am*	**esse**	*to be*

Exercise 21.5

Translate into English:

1. legere amo.

   ....

2. pugnare parant.

   ....

3. pugnare constituunt.

   ....

4. venire non cupit.

   ....

5. respondere parat.

   ....

Exercise 21.6

Translate into Latin:

1. We decide to sail towards the island.

   ....

2. We order the men to build a villa.

   ....

3. Girls never want to be sailors.

   ....

4. The mistress orders the maidservants to work.

   ....

5. The slave orders the horse to run out of the field.

   ....

Handy Help

Conjugation	Present	English	Infinitive	English
1st	amo	*I love*	am**are**	*to love*
2nd	moneo	*I warn*	mon**ere**	*to warn*
3rd	rego	*I rule*	reg**ere**	*to rule*
4th	audio	*I hear*	aud**ire**	*to hear*
irregular verb	sum	*I am*	**esse**	*to be*

Chapter 22
Romulus and Remus: Part 2

Exercise 22.1
Translate the following passage into good English.

Amulius' slaves carry out his cruel orders.

1   Amulius, ubi Romulum et Remum videt, <u>iratus</u> est. pueros

<u>parvos</u> statim necare constituit. Amulius <u>igitur</u> servos vocat.

servos pueros <u>capere</u> iubet. servos pueros ad <u>fluvium</u>

portare iubet. servos pueros in aquam <u>iacere</u> iubet. servi

5   <u>tamen</u>, quod pueros amant, <u>hoc</u> <u>facere</u> non cupiunt. sed

Amulium timent. Amulium magnopere timent. pueros <u>igitur</u>

<u>capiunt,</u> <u>eos</u> ad <u>fluvium</u> portant, <u>eos</u> in aquam <u>iaciunt.</u>

<u>deinde</u> discedunt.

iratus = angry

parvos = little
igitur = therefore

capio (3½) = I take, capture
fluvius = river
iacio (3½) = I throw

tamen = however
hoc = this (acusative)
facio (3½) = I do, make

eos = themselves

deinde = then, next

(A copy of this passage in workbook format can be found on page 111.)

Exercise 22.2
1.   From the passage above give, in Latin, an example of:
     a. an infinitive;
     b. a preposition;
     c. a conjunction.

2.   **videt** (line 1). Give the Latin subject of this verb.

3.   **vocat** (line 2). Give the Latin object of this verb.

4.   **fluvium** (line 3). In which case is this noun? Why is this case used?

5.   **cupiunt** (line 5). Give the person and number of this verb.

6.   **portant** (line 7). Explain the connection between this word and the English word *portable*.

Vocabulary Box 16a		Vocabulary Box 16b	
deinde	then, next	however	tamen
igitur	therefore	then, next	deinde
tamen	however	therefore	igitur
capio (3½)	I take, capture	I do, make	facio (3½)
facio (3½)	I do, make	I take, capture	capio (3½)
iacio (3½)	I throw	I throw	iacio (3½)

As you will see from lines 4 and 5 of the passage, 3½ verbs, though behaving like *audio* (4), have their infinitives (*to*-words) in -*ere*, not the -*ire* you might expect. Other text books will mark these verbs 3, or 4-ish, or 5, or more often M, standing for 'mixed conjugation'.

Chapter 23
Neuter nouns like *bellum*

You will be pleased to hear that this is the final noun type you will need to know for Common Entrance Level 1.

The nouns you have met so far have been either feminine (like *puella*) or masculine (like *servus* and similar nouns). This new noun type is neuter in gender. Neuter simply means 'neither'. Study carefully the table of *bellum* (war) below. It is probably the easiest noun table you will ever learn!

case	job	*bellum* (war) n.
SINGULAR		
nominative	subject (doer)	bell**um**
vocative	person spoken to	bell**um**
accusative	object (receiver)	bell**um**
genitive	*of the*	bell**i**
dative	*to* or *for*	bell**o**
ablative	*by* or *with* or *from*	bell**o**
PLURAL		
nominative	subjects (doers)	bell**a**
vocative	persons spoken to	bell**a**
accusative	objects (receivers)	bell**a**
genitive	*of the*	bell**orum**
dative	*to* or *for*	bell**is**
ablative	*by* or *with* or *from*	bell**is**

Things to note:
- Neuter nouns of this type end in *-um*.
- Their nominatives, vocatives and accusatives are the same.
- Their nominative, vocative and accusative plurals always end in *-a*.
- (Beware of confusing these with *puella*-type nouns which have their <u>singular</u> in *-a*.)
- Their genitives, datives and ablatives are the same as those of *servus*.

Vocabulary box 17 below contains all the neuter nouns you will need to know for Common Entrance Level 1.

Vocabulary Box 17a

aurum	gold
auxilium	help
bellum	war
caelum	sky
consilium (see Note 1 below)	plan
forum (see Note 2 below)	forum, market place
oppidum	town
periculum	danger
proelium	battle
scutum	shield
templum	temple
verbum	word
vinum	wine

Vocabulary Box 17b

battle	proelium
danger	periculum
forum, market place	forum (see Note 2 below)
gold	aurum
help	auxilium
plan	consilium (see Note 1 below)
shield	scutum
sky	caelum
! temple	templum
! town	oppidum
war	bellum
! wine	vinum
word	verbum

Note 1
Note the phrase *consilium capio*, I form a plan.

Note 2
A forum was the open space in the centre of a town where people would meet to socialise, discuss public affairs, and buy and sell things.

Exercise 23.1

Translate into English:

1. servi scuta habent.

   ....

2. in foro stamus.

   ....

3. agricolae bella semper timent.

   ....

4. serve, cur aurum portas?

   ....

5. vinum domini numquam bibimus.

   ....

6. viri servos in bello saepe necant.

   ....

7. nautae muros oppidi oppugnant.

   ....

8. auxilio servorum villam aedificamus.

   ....

9. poeta librum in templo scribit.

   ....

10. verba magistri numquam audimus.

   ....

Exercise 23.2

Translate into Latin:

1. We fear the dangers of war.

   ....

2. Girls do not carry shields.

   ....

3. Farmers, why are you looking at the sky?

   ....

4. Men do not give wine to boys.

   ....

5. The man hurries out of the temple into the forum.

   ....

Exercise 23.3

Translate into English:

1. incolae aurum ex templo portant.

....

2. vinum in villa saepe bibimus.

....

3. incolae, cur auxilium rogatis?

....

4. magistri pueros et puellas verbis saepe terrent.

....

5. dominus auxilium ad servos mittit.

....

6. dominae aurum ancillis non saepe dant.

....

7. verba magistrorum puellas saepe terrent.

....

8. dominus aurum habere amat.

....

9. dominus ancillam de muro iacit.

....

10. puella, cur in templo dormis?

....

Exercise 23.4

Translate into Latin:

1. I like wine.

....

2. Towns are on the island.

....

3. The slaves are running out of the battle.

....

4. We are looking at the temples of the town.

....

5. Why are men fighting in the forum?

....

Chapter 24
Revision

You have now met all the noun types you need to know for Common Entrance Level 1, so this is a good time to consolidate and revise these.

case	job	puella (girl) f.	servus (slave) m.	puer (boy) m.	ager (field) m.	vir (man) m.	bellum (war) n.
			1st declension → puella, then **2nd declension** → servus, puer, ager, vir, bellum				
SINGULAR							
nominative	subject (doer)	puella	servus	puer	ager	vir	bellum
vocative	person spoken to	puella	serve	puer	ager	vir	bellum
accusative	object (receiver)	puellam	servum	puerum	agrum	virum	bellum
genitive	*of the*	puellae	servi	pueri	agri	viri	belli
dative	*to* or *for*	puellae	servo	puero	agro	viro	bello
ablative	*by* or *with* or *from*	puella	servo	puero	agro	viro	bello
PLURAL							
nominative	subjects (doers)	puellae	servi	pueri	agri	viri	bella
vocative	persons spoken to	puellae	servi	pueri	agri	viri	bella
accusative	objects (receivers)	puellas	servos	pueros	agros	viros	bella
genitive	*of the*	puellarum	servorum	puerorum	agrorum	virorum	bellorum
dative	*to* or *for*	puellis	servis	pueris	agris	viris	bellis
ablative	*by* or *with* or *from*	puellis	servis	pueris	agris	viris	bellis

The seven *servus*-type nouns listed below complete all the nouns you need to know for Level 1. A complete listing can be found on the next page, as well as in the Reference Section starting on page 121.

Vocabulary Box 18a	
captivus	prisoner
hortus	garden
libertus	freedman, ex-slave
locus	place
nuntius	messenger
socius	ally, comrade
ventus	wind

Vocabulary Box 18b	
ally, comrade	socius
freedman, ex-slave	libertus
garden	hortus
messenger	nuntius
place	locus
prisoner	captivus
wind	ventus

Level 1 Noun Checklist

Below is a complete list of the nouns prescribed for Level 1.
Here is a reminder about how nouns are set out in word lists (see page 39 for a fuller explanation):

nominative singular, genitive singular, gender, English meaning

ager, agri m.	field	forum, -i n.	forum	puella, -ae f.	girl
agricola, -ae m.	farmer	gladius, -i m.	sword	puer, -i m.	boy
amicus, -i m.	friend	Graecia, -i f.	Greece	regina, ae f.	queen
ancilla, -ae f.	slave-girl	hasta, -ae f.	spear	Roma, -ae f.	Rome
aqua, -ae f.	water	hortus, -i m.	garden	sagitta, -ae f.	arrow
aurum, -i n.	gold	incola, -ae m.	inhabitant	scutum, -i n.	shield
auxilium, -i n.	help	insula, -ae f.	island	servus, -i m.	slave-girl
bellum, -i n.	war	ira, -ae f.	anger	silva, -a f.	wood
caelum, -i n.	sky	liber, libri m.	book	socius, -i m.	comrade
captivus, -i m.	prisoner	libertus, -i m.	freedman	templum, -i n.	temple
cena, -ae f.	dinner	locus, -i m.	place	terra, -ae f.	land
cibus, -i m.	food	magister, -tri m.	teacher	Troia, -ae f.	Troy
consilium, -i n.	plan	maritus, -i m.	husband	turba, -ae f.	crowd
dea, -ae f.	goddess	murus, -i m.	wall	unda, -ae f.	wave
deus, -i m.	god	nauta, -ae m.	sailor	ventus, -i m.	wind
domina, -ae f.	mistress	nuntius, -i m.	messenger	verbum, -i n.	word
dominus, -i m.	master	oppidum, -i n.	town	via, -ae f.	road
epistula, -ae f.	letter	patria, -ae f.	homeland	villa, -ae f.	villa
equus, -i m.	horse	pecunia, -ae f.	money	vinum, -i n.	wine
femina, -ae f.	woman	periculum, -i n.	danger	vir, -i m.	man
filia, -ae f.	daughter	poeta, -ae m.	poet		
filius, -i m.	son	proelium, -i n.	battle		

Exercise 24.1

Translate into English:

1. nautae ventos non timent.

2. hortos insulae spectamus.

3. libertus domini pecuniam amat.

4. pecuniam liberto numquam do.

5. ancillae ex villa in hortum festinant.

6. domini aurum libertis non saepe dant.

7. auxilio sociorum Troiam oppugnamus.

8. cur pecuniam captivis das, domine?

9. captivi consilium in templo capiunt.

10. socii incolas Romae hastis et gladiis necant.

Exercise 24.2

Translate into Latin:

1. We like gardens.

   ....

2. The slaves are running out of the place.

   ....

3. The prisoner frightens the girls.

   ....

4. Prisoners do not read books.

   ....

5. The queen often gives help to the allies.

   ....

6. The girl is writing a letter in the garden.

   ....

7. The girls are writing letters in the gardens.

   ....

8. Why are you praising the prisoner, slave?

   ....

9. The allies are giving help to the inhabitants.

   ....

10. We often take prisoners in war.

    ....

Exercise 24.3

Translate into Latin:

1. The messenger is running towards the town.

   ....

2. The slaves are working in the garden.

   ....

3. Winds and waves do not frighten sailors.

   ....

4. The freedman lives with his master in Greece.

   ....

5. Allies never fight with the inhabitants of the land.

   ....

Chapter 25
Romulus and Remus: Part 3

Exercise 25.1
Translate into English.

Romulus and Remus are saved by the gods.

1   Romulus et Remus in <u>fluvio</u> iam sunt. aquam

    magnopere timent. aqua pueros per <u>fluvium</u> portat.

    in <u>magno</u> periculo sunt. dei tamen, ubi <u>parvos</u>

    pueros in <u>fluvio</u> vident, <u>eos</u> <u>servare</u> constituunt.

5   undae pueros ad terram <u>mox</u> portant et <u>ibi</u> <u>ponunt</u>.

    pueri, quod <u>fessi</u> sunt, in terra dormiunt. <u>ibi</u> diu

    <u>manent</u>. <u>itaque</u> Romulus et Remus iam <u>tuti</u> sunt.

fluvius = river

magnus = great, big
parvos = small, little
eos = them
servo (1) = I save
mox = soon
ibi = there
pono (3) = I put
fessi = tired
maneo (2) = I stay, remain
itaque = and so
tuti = safe

(A copy of this passage in workbook format can be found on page 112.)

Exercise 25.2
Answer these questions. They are based on the passage above. Complete English sentences are not required.

1.   From the passage, give, in Latin, one example of each of the following:
     a.   a feminine noun;
     b.   a second conjugation verb;
     c.   a conjunction;
     d.   an adverb.

2.   **aqua** (line 2). Explain the connection between this word and the English word *aquarium*.

3.   **sunt** (line 3). Give the first person singular of this verb.

4.   **pueros** (line 5). Give the case and number of this noun.

5.   **dormiunt** (line 6). Give the Latin subject of this verb.

Vocabulary Box 19a	
maneo (2)	I stay, remain
pono (3)	I put, place
ibi	there
itaque	and so, therefore
mox	soon
sic	thus, in this way

Vocabulary Box 19b	
I put, place	pono (3)
I stay, remain	maneo (2)
and so, therefore	itaque
soon	mox
there	ibi
thus, in this way	sic

Chapter 26
Adjectives like *bonus*

Adjectives are words which describe nouns. English examples are *small, happy, angry, beautiful, many, big, tired*.

You may have spotted in recent reading passages some Latin adjectives, like *magna* (big), *multi* (many), *laeti* (happy), *Romanus* (Roman), *fessi* (tired), *pulchra* (beautiful), *iratus* (angry), *parvi* (small).

An adjective in Latin has different endings, according to the noun which it is describing. More of this later. First, look at the different endings in the table of *bonus* (good) below. Where have you met these endings before?

number	case	masculine	feminine	neuter
		GENDER		
SINGULAR	nominative	bon**us**	bon**a**	bon**um**
	vocative	bon**e**	bon**a**	bon**um**
	accusative	bon**um**	bon**am**	bon**um**
	genitive	bon**i**	bon**ae**	bon**i**
	dative	bon**o**	bon**ae**	bon**o**
	ablative	bon**o**	bon**a**	bon**o**
PLURAL	nominative	bon**i**	bon**ae**	bon**a**
	vocative	bon**i**	bon**ae**	bon**a**
	accusative	bon**os**	bon**as**	bon**a**
	genitive	bon**orum**	bon**arum**	bon**orum**
	dative	bon**is**	bon**is**	bon**is**
	ablative	bon**is**	bon**is**	bon**is**

Things to note:
- The masculine endings are the same as those of *servus* (second declension).
- The feminine endings are the same as those of *puella* (first declension).
- The neuter endings are the same as those of *bellum*. (second declension).

(Some textbooks refer to these kind of adjectives as 2-1-2 adjectives, because the masculine/feminine/neuter endings are the same as these noun declensions).

Listings

When adjectives are listed in dictionaries or wordlists, you will find three words given:
The first word is the nominative <u>masculine</u> singular.
The second word is the nominative <u>feminine</u> singular ending.
The third word is the nominative <u>neuter</u> singular ending.

Vocabulary Box 20a	
bonus, -a, -um	good
clarus, -a, -um	famous, clear, bright
fessus, -a, -um	tired
Graecus, -a, -um	Greek
iratus, -a, -um	angry
laetus, -a, -um	happy
magnus, -a, -um	great, big
malus, -a, -um	bad, evil, wicked
multi, -ae, -a (plural endings)	many, much
parvus, -a, -um	small, little
Romanus, -a, -um	Roman
Troianus, -a, -um	Trojan
tutus, -a, -um	safe

Vocabulary Box 20b	
angry	iratus, -a, -um
bad, evil, wicked	malus, -a, -um
great, big	magnus, -a, -um
famous, clear, bright	clarus, -a, -um
good	bonus, -a, -um
Greek	Graecus, -a, -um
happy	laetus, -a, -um
many, much	multi, -ae, -a (plural endings)
! Roman	Romanus, -a, -um
safe	tutus, -a, -um
small, little	parvus, -a, -um
tired	fessus, -a, -um
Trojan	Troianus, -a, -um

'Agreement'

An adjective must have the same gender, case and number as the noun it is describing. This is called 'agreement' – the adjective must agree with its noun. Study the following examples. The adjective sometimes comes <u>after</u> the noun it is describing (adjectives of quantity or size usually come <u>before</u> the noun they are describing).

servus iratus clamat.	*The angry slave is shouting.*	(masculine singular)
servi irati clamant.	*The angry slaves are shouting.*	(masculine plural)
puella laeta cantat.	*The happy girl is singing.*	(feminine singular)
puellae laetae cantant.	*The happy girls are singing.*	(feminine plural)
oppidum est magnum.	*The town is big.*	(neuter singular)
oppida sunt magna.	*The towns are big.*	(neuter plural)

Exercise 26.1

Translate into Latin:

1. a small girl
2. small girls
3. a famous man
4. famous men
5. a bad word
6. bad words
7. an angry master
8. angry masters
9. a big temple
10. big temples

Exercise 26.2

Translate into Latin:

1. good wines
2. a safe island
3. safe islands
4. a happy sailor*
5. happy sailors*
6. the angry slave girl
7. angry slave girls
8. many boys (put the Latin for 'many' first)
9. many shields (put the Latin for 'many' first)
10. many arrows (put the Latin for 'many' first)

*Careful! Sailor in Latin is masculine, despite having endings like *puella*.

Exercise 26.3

Translate into English:

1. multi pueri numquam laborant.

   ....

2. vina bona saepe bibo.

   ....

3. magistri mali saepe sunt.

   ....

4. magnas turbas timeo.

   ....

5. poetam clarum laudamus.

   ....

6. pueri parvi iam tuti sunt.

   ....

7. bonum librum legimus.

   ....

8. multas hastas iaciunt.

   ....

9. agricola multos agros habet.

   ....

10. nautae magnas undas timent.

    ....

Exercise 26.4

Translate into Latin:

1. I have a good husband.

   ....

2. You (pl) are building a big temple.

   ....

3. They praise the famous queen.

   ....

4. We have good allies.

   ....

5. She praises the good slave-girls.

   ....

Exercise 26.5

Translate into English:

1. servi fessi semper bene dormiunt.

   ....

2. muri oppidi magni sunt.

   ....

3. magni venti multos nautas terrent.

   ....

4. pueri verba irati magistri audiunt.

   ....

5. pueri verba irata magistri audiunt.

   ....

6. multos amicos bonos non habeo.

   ....

7. fessi sumus quod magnum murum aedificamus.

   ....

8. socii multos captivos in proelio capiunt.

   ....

9. domini pecuniam servis bonis saepe dant.

   ....

10. turba incolarum iratorum ad forum festinat.

   ....

Exercise 26.6

Translate into Latin:

1. The teacher warns the bad boys.

   ....

2. The good queen has a happy son and a happy daughter.

   ....

3. The slaves are tired because they are always working.

   ....

4. Many men are fighting against the slaves in the streets.

   ....

5. The maidservants are preparing a good dinner for the famous man.

   ....

Chapter 27
Romulus and Remus: Part 4

Exercise 27.1
Translate into English.

Romulus and Remus are helped by a she-wolf and a woodpecker.

1 Romulus et Remus in terra sunt. pueri aquam bibunt, sed
cibum non habent. in magno periculo igitur <u>adhuc</u> sunt.
prope <u>fluvium</u> habitat <u>lupa</u>. <u>lupa</u>, ubi prope <u>fluvium</u>
ambulat, <u>subito duos</u> pueros parvos videt. <u>eos servare</u>
5 constituit. Romulum et Remum <u>domum</u> portat. <u>lupa</u>
amicum bonum habet. amicus <u>lupae</u> est <u>picus</u>. <u>lupa</u> et
<u>picus</u> pueros diu <u>curant</u>. <u>lupa lac</u>, <u>picus</u> cibum Romulo et
Remo dat. pueri iam tuti et laeti sunt.

adhuc = still
fluvius = river
lupa = she-wolf
subito = suddenly
duos = two
eos = them
servo (1) = I save
domum = (to) home
picus = woodpecker
curo (1) = I look after
lac = milk

(A copy of this passage in workbook format can be found on page 113.)

Exercise 27.2
Answer these questions. They are based on the passage above. Complete English sentences are not required.

1. From the passage, give, in Latin, one example of each of the following:
   a. a first conjugation verb;
   b. a second conjugation verb;
   c. a third conjugation verb;
   d. an adverb.

2. **bibunt** (line 1). Give the Latin object of this verb.

3. **habitat** (line 3). Explain the connection between this word and the English word *uninhabitable*

4. **amicus** (line 6). Give the gender of this noun.

5. **Romulo** (line 7). Give the case of this noun.

Vocabulary Box 21a	
unus	one
duo	two
tres	three
quattuor	four
quinque	five
sex	six
septem	seven
octo	eight
novem	nine
decem	ten

Vocabulary Box 21b	
one	unus
two	duo
three	tres
four	quattuor
five	quinque
six	sex
seven	septem
eight	octo
nine	novem
ten	decem

Chapter 28
The Imperfect Tense

'Tense' means 'time', and refers to when an action (verb) takes place.
Actions take place in past time, present time or future time.

All the verbs we have met so far describe actions which are going on at the moment; in other words, they are happening in the present.

For example:	ambulat.	*He is walking.*
	dormiunt.	*They are sleeping.*

These verbs are said to be in the present tense.

We are about to meet a couple of tenses which relate to actions taking place in the past. You will meet them a lot. There is no single past tense in Latin.

The first of these tenses is called the **imperfect tense**.

This tense is not called the imperfect because there is something wrong with it!

'Imperfect' actually means 'incomplete' or 'not finished.' It describes a continuous action or a habit in the past – something which happened not just once, but over a period of time.

There are several options when it comes to translating these into good English.

Here are some English examples:
> The boy **was** walking.
> The poets **were** writing.
> The slave **used to** work hard.
> He **would** go to football every Saturday.

In Latin the personal endings of these verbs are:

-bam	I was doing / I used to do something
-bas	You were doing / You used to do something
-bat	He/She/It was doing/ He/She/It used to do something
-bamus	We were doing / We used to do something
-batis	You were doing / You used to do something
-bant	They were doing / used to do something

These endings are linked to the verb stems by a vowel or two, as you will see in the following table. The verb 'to be' of course is, as usual, irregular – but it's very common!

When it comes to translating these into English, look at the context and decide which option sounds most natural. Remember, the options are:
> was doing something
> were doing something
> used to do something
> would do something

The Imperfect Tense

person	number	English	1 **amo** *loving*	2 **moneo** *warning*	key endings
1st	singular	*I was*	amabam	monebam	**-bam**
2nd	singular	*You were*	amabas	monebas	**-bas**
3rd	singular	*He was*	amabat	monebat	**-bat**
1st	plural	*We were*	amabamus	monebamus	**-bamus**
2nd	plural	*You were*	amabatis	monebatis	**-batis**
3rd	plural	*They were*	amabant	monebant	**-bant**

person	number	English	3 **rego** *ruling*	4 **audio** *hearing*	
1st	singular	*I was*	regebam	audiebam	**-bam**
2nd	singular	*You were*	regebas	audiebas	**-bas**
t3rd	singular	*He was*	regebat	audiebat	**-bat**
1st	plural	*We were*	regebamus	audiebamus	**-bamus**
2nd	plural	*You were*	regebatis	audiebatis	**-batis**
3rd	plural	*They were*	regebant	audiebant	**-bant**

Irregular verb: sum (*to be*)				
(high priority for learning – these are so common in CE papers!)				
				was/were
1st	singular	eram		*I was*
2nd	singular	eras		*You were*
3rd	singular	erat		*He/She/It was*
1st	plural	eramus		*We were*
2nd	plural	eratis		*You were*
3rd	plural	erant		*They were*

Exercise 28.1

Translate into Latin:

1. He was living.
2. I was holding.
3. They were drinking.
4. You (sg) were sleeping.
5. We were.
6. They used to live.
7. She was moving.
8. We were reading.
9. You (pl) were coming.
10. He was.

Exercise 28.2

Translate into Latin:

1. They used to fight.
2. I was watching.
3. We were putting.
4. She was departing.
5. You (pl) were frightening.
6. They used to drink.
7. We were running.
8. He was listening.
9. You (sg) were leading.
10. They were ordering.

Exercise 28.3

Translate into English:

1. ponebat.
2. manebant.
3. discedebant.
4. constituebat.
5. eram.
6. stabant.
7. bibebam.
8. clamabatis.
9. discedebamus.
10. mittebam.

Exercise 28.4

Translate into English:

1. bibebamus.
2. scribebatis.
3. movebant.
4. stabat.
5. eramus.
6. navigabant.
7. tenebas.
8. aedificabat.
9. videbam.
10. iubebat.

Exercise 28.5

Translate into Latin:

1. The Trojans were fighting bravely.

2. The inhabitant was walking along the road.

3. The farmers were carrying shields.

4. The slave girl used to have money.

5. The boy would often drink water.

Exercise 28.6

Translate into Latin:

1. The men were attacking the island.

   ....

2. The slaves were throwing arrows.

   ....

3. The farmers were not afraid of (= were not fearing) the gods.

   ....

4. Women did not used to like wars.

   ....

5. The girls used to like the farmer.

   ....

Exercise 28.7

Translate into Latin:

1. Many sailors were sleeping in the Greek temple.

   ....

2. The slaves were leading the small horses into the field.

   ....

3. The bad boy was frightening many girls with (his) big sword.

   ....

Exercise 28.8

Translate into English:

1. domina filium et filiam habebat.

2. fessi eramus quod murum aedificabamus.

3. ancilla cenam bonam parabat.

4. per viam currebatis.

5. magna turba puellas terrebat.

6. ad insulam navigabamus.

7. multi liberti in villa manebant.

8. auxilium veniebat.

9. aquam et vinum bibebam.

10. muros gladiis oppugnabamus.

Exercise 28.9

Translate into English:

1. domina epistulas in horto saepe scribebat.

2. pueri Romani per viam festinabant.

3. magistrum audiebamus.

4. agricola in agris habitabat.

5. regina pecuniam et aurum amabat.

6. servi in templo dormiebant.

7. Troiani hastas et sagittas iaciebant.

8. nautae vinum in foro saepe bibebant.

9. villam aedificabas.

10. femina maritum pecuniam saepe rogabat.

Exercise 28.10

Translate into English:

1. magister pueros malos semper monebat.

2. nautae contra incolas in viis pugnabant.

3. domina ancillas in villam vocabat.

4. verba magistri parvas puellas terrebant.

5. equi ex oppido in agros currebant.

Chapter 29
Romulus and Remus: Part 5

Exercise 29.1
Translate into English.

Faustulus, a shepherd, finds Romulus and Remus.

1   Romulus et Remus cum <u>lupa</u> et <u>pico</u> diu
    <u>manserunt</u>. <u>olim</u> <u>pastor</u>, Faustulus, parvos pueros
    in agris <u>conspexit</u>. ubi <u>eos</u> vidit, <u>attonitus</u> erat. ad
    villam <u>suam</u> <u>cucurrit</u>. <u>hic</u> habitabat Faustulus cum
5   <u>uxore</u>, Acca. Accae <u>clamavit</u>: 'Acca, veni statim!
    curre!' Acca Faustulo <u>respondit</u>: '<u>quid</u> est,
    Faustule? cur clamas? responde!' Faustulus Accae
    <u>respondit</u>: 'duos parvos pueros <u>inveni</u>. in periculo
    sunt.' Acca Faustulo <u>respondit</u>: '<u>ubi</u> sunt,
10 Faustule?' Faustulus <u>iterum</u> <u>clamavit</u>: 'in agris sunt.
    veni! festina!' itaque Faustulus et Acca ad agros
    statim <u>festinaverunt</u>. ibi Romulum et Remum
    <u>invenerunt</u> et ad villam <u>duxerunt</u>.

lupa	= wolf
picus	= woodpecker
manserunt	= (they) stayed
olim	= one day
pastor	= shepherd
conspexit	= (he) caught sight of
eos	= them
attonitus	= amazed
suus	= his
cucurrit	= he ran
hic	= here
uxore	= wife
clamavit	= he shouted
respondit	= (she/he) replied
quid?	= what?
inveni	= I have found
ubi?	= where?
iterum	= again
festinaverunt	= (they hurried)
invenerunt	= they found
duxerunt	= they led

(A copy of this passage in workbook format can be found on page 114.)

Exercise 29.2
Answer these questions. They are based on the passage above. Complete English sentences are not required.

1. From the passage, give, in Latin, one example of each of the following:
   a. a first conjugation verb;
   b. a preposition;
   c. a part of the verb *to be*;
   d. an adverb.
2. **agris** (line 3). Explain the connection between this word and the English word *agriculture.*
3. **habitabat** (line 4). Give the person and number of this verb.
4. **Accae** (line 5). Give the case of this noun.
5. **respondit** (line 8). Give the Latin subject of this verb.

Vocabulary Box 22a	
duco (3)	I lead
hic	here
iterum	again
olim	one day
quid?	what?
suus, -a, -um	his, her, their
ubi?	where?

Vocabulary Box 22b	
again	iterum
here	hic
his, her, their	suus, -a, -um
I lead	duco (3)
one day	olim
what?	quid?
where?	ubi

Chapter 30
Imperatives: giving orders

In Exercise 29.1 we came across Faustulus shouting to his wife:

Acca, **veni** statim! **curre**!   *Acca, **come** immediately! **Run**!*

The words in **bold** are a part of the verb called the **imperative**.

Imperatives are used for giving orders to someone.

In Latin, giving orders to one person is expressed by a singular imperative; giving orders to more than one person is called a plural imperative.

Here is a table of imperatives for all the verb conjugations:

Table of Imperatives

		singular	*plural*	*English*
1	amo (*I like*)	am**a**!	am**ate**!	*Like!*
2	moneo (*I warn*)	mon**e**!	mon**ete**!	*Warn!*
3	rego (*I rule*)	reg**e**!	reg**ite**!	*Rule!*
3½*	capio (*I take*)	cap**e**!	cap**ite**!	*Take!*
4	audio (*I listen, hear*)	aud**i**!	aud**ite**!	*Listen!*
irregulars	sum (*I am*)	**es!** *or* **esto!**	**este!** *or* **estote!**	*Be!*
3	dico (*I say*)	**dic!**	dicite!	*Say!*
3	duco (*I lead*)	**duc!**	ducite!	*Lead!*
3½*	facio (*I do, make*)	**fac!**	facite!	*Do!/Make!*

*3½, or 'mixed conjugation' verbs, behave like 3rd conjugation verbs in some ways (imperatives and infinitives), but like 4th conjugation verbs in others (present and imperfect tenses).

Examples:

audi, serve!	*Listen, slave!*	(singular imperative)
audite, servi!	*Listen, slaves!*	(plural imperative)

Hints
The person(s) being ordered will be in the vocative (person spoken to) case in Latin.
The person being ordered to do something will be separated from what he is being told to do by a comma. This comma is important – do not ignore it.

Boys run. (a statement) is different from *Boys, run!* (an imperative).

Exercise 30.1

Translate into Latin:

1. Rule, queen!

   ....

2. Rule, queens!

   ....

3. Run, boy!

   ....

4. Run, boys!

   ....

5. Attack, friend!

   ....

6. Attack, friends!

   ....

7. Fight, slave!

   ....

8. Fight, slaves!

   ....

9. Sleep, girl!

   ....

10. Sleep, girls!

   ....

Exercise 30.2

Translate into Latin:

1. Drink the wine, boy!

   ....

2. Drink the wine, boys!

   ....

3. Build a wall, slave!

   ....

4. Build a wall, slaves!

   ....

5. Prepare (your) spear, farmer!

   ....

Exercise 30.3

Translate into English:

1. hastas iacite, agricolae!

....

2. scuta parate, servi!

....

3. puer, bonum librum lege!

....

4. semper bene pugnate, Romani!

....

5. incolas necate, nautae!

....

6. pecuniam capite, pueri!

....

7. ancillam malam puni, domina!

....

8. oppidum oppugnate, nautae!

....

9. magnum murum aedifica, serve!

....

10. verba magistri audite, pueri!

....

Exercise 30.4

Translate into Latin:

1. Run across the road, boy!

....

2. Fight well in battle, men!

....

3. Sail away from the island, sailors!

....

4. Write a book in the garden, poet!

....

5. Attack the villa with your spears, slaves!

....

Chapter 31
Romulus and Remus: Part 6

Exercise 31.1
Translate into English.

Romulus and Remus grow up but eventually decide to leave Acca and Faustulus.

1   Romulus et Remus tuti iam erant. in villa Accae et

Faustuli diu <u>habitaverunt</u>. mox parvi pueri <u>iuvenes</u>

erant. <u>tandem</u>, quod suum oppidum <u>novum</u>

aedificare <u>cupiverunt</u>, a villa discedere

5   <u>constituerunt</u>. ad Accam et Faustulum igitur

<u>appropinquaverunt</u> et <u>haec</u> verba <u>dixerunt</u>:

'Acca et Faustule, <u>nos vos</u> magnopere amamus.

sed discedere et <u>novum</u> oppidum aedificare

cupimus. oppidum <u>nostrum</u> magnum et <u>pulchrum</u>

10   et <u>notum erit</u>.'

habitaverunt = they lived
iuvenes = young men
tandem = at last, finally
novus = new
cupiverunt = they wanted

constituerunt = they decided

appropinquaverunt = they approached
haec = these
dixerunt = (they) said
nos = we
vos = you (accusative)

noster = our
pulcher = beautiful
notus = well known
erit = (it) will be

(A copy of this passage in workbook format can be found on page 115.)

Exercise 31.2
Answer these questions. They are based on the passage above. Complete English sentences are not required.

1. From the passage, give, in Latin, one example of each of the following:
    a. an adverb;
    b. an infinitive;
    c. a preposition;
    d. a neuter noun.

2. **erant** (line 1). In what tense is this verb? Give the first person singular of the present tense of this verb.

3. **Accae** (line 1). Give the case of this noun.

4. **dixerunt** (line 6). Give the Latin object of this verb.

5. **Faustule** (line 7). Give the case of this noun.

6. **cupimus** (line 9). Give the person of this verb.

Chapter 32
Adjectives in -er; *You* and *I*

You have already met the adjective *bonus – good*. Two further groups of adjectives behave in more or less the same way, except that their masculine endings go like *puer* or *ager*. Compare these two tables:

miser *(miserable, wretched)*

| number | case | | GENDER | |
		masculine	feminine	neuter
SINGULAR	nominative (subject)	miser	misera	miserum
	vocative (spoken to)	miser	misera	miserum
	accusative (object)	miserum	miseram	miserum
	genitive ('of')	miseri	miserae	miseri
	dative ('to'/'for')	misero	miserae	misero
	ablative ('by'/'with'/'from')	misero	misera	misero
PLURAL	nominative (subjects)	miseri	miserae	misera
	vocative (spoken to)	miseri	miserae	misera
	accusative (objects)	miseros	miseras	misera
	genitive ('of')	miserorum	miserarum	miserorum
	dative ('to'/'for')	miseris	miseris	miseris
	ablative ('by'/'with'/'from')	miseris	miseris	miseris

pulcher *(beautiful, handsome)*
(this drops the letter *e* after the masculine vocative singular, just like *ager*.)

| number | case | | GENDER | |
		masculine	feminine	neuter
SINGULAR	nominative (subject)	pulcher	pulchra	pulchrum
	vocative (spoken to)	pulcher	pulchra	pulchrum
	accusative (object)	pulchrum	pulchram	pulchrum
	genitive ('of')	pulchri	pulchrae	pulchri
	dative ('to'/'for')	pulchro	pulchrae	pulchro
	ablative ('by'/'with'/'from')	pulchro	pulchra	pulchro
PLURAL	nominative (subjects)	pulchri	pulchrae	pulchra
	vocative (spoken to)	pulchri	pulchrae	pulchra
	accusative (objects)	pulchros	pulchras	pulchra
	genitive ('of')	pulchrorum	pulchrarum	pulchrorum
	dative ('to'/'for')	pulchris	pulchris	pulchris
	ablative ('by'/'with'/'from')	pulchris	pulchris	pulchris

Vocabulary Box 23a	
miser, misera, miserum	miserable
noster, nostra, nostrum	our
notus, -a, -um	well known
novus, -a, -um	new
pulcher, pulchra, pulchrum	beautiful
vester, vestra, vestrum	your (pl)

Vocabulary Box 23b	
beautiful	pulcher, pulchra, pulchrum
miserable	miser, misera, miserum
new	novus, -a, -um
our	noster, nostra, nostrum
well known	notus, -a, -um
your (pl)	vester, vestra, vestrum

Exercise 32.1

Translate into Latin:

1. A miserable slave.
2. Miserable slaves.
3. A beautiful girl.
4. Beautiful girls.
5. A miserable farmer.
6. Miserable farmers.
7. A beautiful horse.
8. Beautiful horses.
9. A miserable war.
10. Miserable wars

Exercise 32.2

Translate into Latin:

1. Your (pl) money.
2. Our money.
3. Your (pl) books.
4. Our books.
5. Your (pl) shields.
6. Our shields.
7. Your (pl) master.
8. Our masters.
9. Your (pl) slaves.
10. Our arrows.

Exercise 32.3

Translate into Latin:

1. I have a miserable slave girl.
2. I am looking at the beautiful garden.
3. I see your (pl) horses.
4. I like our master.
5. I drink beautiful wines.

Exercise 32.4

Translate into Latin:

1. I used to have a beautiful villa.
2. He was reading a good book.
3. We were looking at the beautiful temples.
4. I was not praising the miserable slavegirls.
5. They were destroying the beautiful forum.

Exercise 32.5

Translate into English:

1. regina nostros socios saepe laudabat.
2. miseri servi ex templo pulchro currebant.
3. agricolae, socii vestras villas oppugnant et vestros agros delent!
4. domini, cur servos vestros numquam laudatis?
5. vina bona in horto nostro saepe bibebamus.

You and *I*

You will find these words referred to in grammar books as first person pronouns (*I, we*) and second person pronouns (*you*).

		first person		second person	
singular	nominative	ego	*I*	tu	*you*
	accusative	me	*me*	te	*you*
plural	nominative	nos	*we*	vos	*you*
	accusative	nos	*us*	vos	*you*

The nominatives of these pronouns are somemtimes used to add extra emphasis or to point out a contrast.

Examples

dominus servum laudabat. **ego** servum non laudabam.
*The master was praising the slave. **I** was not praising the slave.*

ego ambulo, sed **tu** curris.
***I** am walking, but **you** are running.*

vos discedebatis, **nos** manebamus.
***You** were departing, **we** were staying.*

Exercise 32.6

Translate into Latin:

1. The girl likes me.
2. The master likes us.
3. I like you (sg).
4. They like us.
5. They do not like you (pl).
6. The queen is watching us.
7. The master hears you (sg).
8. The poet praises you (pl).
9. The mistress is ordering us.
10. I am asking you (sg).

Exercise 32.7

Translate into English:

1. tu puella bona es, ego puella mala sum.
2. ego hastas tenebam, tu sagittas tenebas.
3. ego te amo, sed tu me non amas.
4. socii, vos amamus!
5. vos currebatis, nos ambulabamus.
6. ego miser sum quod puellae me non amant.
7. vos ancillae malae estis, ego domina bona sum.
8. pueri me semper spectant quod ego puella pulchra sum.
9. cur magister me numquam laudabat?
10. magister te numquam laudabat quod tu numquam laborabas.

Chapter 33
Romulus and Remus: Part 7

Exercise 33.1
Translate into English.

The gods give Romulus and Remus some guidance.

1   Romulus et Remus et amici ad <u>fluvium</u> <u>venerunt</u>.

    <u>nomen</u> <u>fluvii</u> erat <u>Tiberis</u>. pueri et amici suum

    oppidum novum in <u>hoc</u> loco aedificare <u>constituerunt</u>.

    prope <u>fluvium</u> erant septem <u>colles</u>. Romulus <u>primum</u>

5   <u>collem</u>, Remus <u>secundum</u> <u>collem</u> <u>ascendit</u>. pueri iam

    fessi erant. hic <u>steterunt</u> et <u>signum</u> deorum

    <u>exspectaverunt</u>. non diu <u>exspectaverunt</u>. Remus sex

    <u>aquilas</u> in caelo <u>conspexit</u>. ubi <u>aquilas</u> <u>vidit</u>, laetus

    erat. <u>risit</u>. deinde Romulus <u>duodecim</u> <u>aquilas</u> in caelo

10   <u>conspexit</u>. ubi <u>aquilas</u> <u>vidit</u>, laetus erat. <u>risit</u>.

fluvius, -i m. = river
venerunt = (they) came
nomen = name
Tiberis = the Tiber
hoc = this
constituerunt = (they) decided

colles = hills
primus, -a, -um = first
collem = hill
secundus, -a, -um = second
ascendit = (he) climbed
steterunt = they stood
signum, -i n. = signal
exspectaverunt = they waited for

aquila, -ae f. = eagle
conspexit = (he) caught sight of
vidit = he saw
risit = he laughed
duodecim = twelve

(A copy of this passage in workbook format can be found on page 116.)

Exercise 33.2

1. From the passage, give, in Latin, an example of:
   a. a conjunction;
   b. an infinitive;
   c. a part of the verb *to be*;
   d. an adverb;
   e. a neuter noun.

2. **fluvium** (line 1). In what case is this noun? Why is this case used?

3. **deorum** (line 6). Give the gender of this noun.

4. **conspexit** (line 8). Give the Latin subject of this verb.

5. **vidit** (line 10). Give the Latin object of this verb.

Chapter 34
The Perfect Tense

Please read and study this page carefully – this is a key topic!

I hope you remember the imperfect tense (the one with the **-bam, -bas, -bat, -bamus, -batis, -bant** endings) and that it indicates a continuous action in the past, e.g. *He was laughing, They were playing, I used to run.* Imperfect means 'not completed'.

In the reading passages about Romulus and Remus we have already met verbs like:

respondit	*He replied*
cucurrit	*He ran*
manserunt	*They stayed*
cupiverunt	*They wanted*

These verbs describe a single, one-off event which happened in the past. This is the Perfect Tense. 'Perfect' means 'completed.' You will meet this tense more than any other in your reading of Latin stories.

In English, a lot of verbs express this single action in the past by adding a *-ed* to the verb stem. For example: *I play* becomes *I played*, or He shouts becomes *He shouted*. There are of course plenty of irregular verbs in English: the past of *I hold* is *I held*, not *I holded*, and the past of *I go* is I went, not *I goed*! There are many others, of course. It's the same in Latin: some forms of the perfect tense are not what you would expect.

However, in Latin the personal endings of the perfect tense are always the same – even for irregular verbs!:

-i	*I (did something)*
-isti	*You (sg) (did something)*
-it	*He /She / It (did something)*
-imus	*We (did something)*
-istis	*You (pl) (did something)*
-erunt	*They (did something)*

It is easy to spot these perfect tense endings when translating out of Latin, but it is not so easy going into Latin. The endings are the same, but the front bit of the verb (the 'stem' – the bit you have to stick the ending on to) is not always obvious.

Study the table of the perfect tenses of all the conjugations on the next page, and you will see what I mean.

person	number	English	1: amo *loved*	2: moneo *warned*
1st person	singular	*I*	amav**i**	monu**i**
2nd person	singular	*You*	amav**isti**	monu**isti**
3rd person	singular	*He/She/It*	amav**it**	monu**it**
1st person	plural	*We*	amav**imus**	monu**imus**
2nd person	plural	*You*	amav**istis**	monu**istis**
3rd person	plural	*They*	amav**erunt**	monu**erunt**

			3: rego *ruled*	4: audio *heard*
1st person	singular	*I*	rex**i**	audiv**i**
2nd person	singular	*You*	rex**isti**	audiv**isti**
3rd person	singular	*He/She/It*	rex**it**	audiv**it**
1st person	plural	*We*	rex**imus**	audiv**imus**
2nd person	plural	*You*	rex**istis**	audiv**istis**
3rd person	plural	*They*	rex**erunt**	audiv**erunt**

			irregular verb: sum *was/were*		key endings
1st person	singular	*I*	fu**i**	*I was*	**-I**
2nd person	singular	*You*	fu**isti**	*You were*	**-ISTI**
3rd person	singular	*He/She/It*	fu**it**	*He was*	**-IT**
1st person	plural	*We*	fu**imus**	*We were*	**-IMUS**
2nd person	plural	*You*	fu**istis**	*You were*	**-ISTIS**
3rd person	plural	*They*	fu**erunt**	*They were*	**-ERUNT**

You will see that the perfect stems (front bits) of the verb conjugations are not what you might expect:

1	amav-	NOT am-
2	monu-	NOT mon- or mone-
3	rex-	NOT reg-
4	audiv-	NOT aud- or audi-
to be	fu-	(very strange, as usual!)

How are you supposed to know what these irregular perfect stems are? Well, you just have to look them up, and try to memorise them. Which brings us to the topic of looking up verbs in wordlists and dictionaries.

So far in this book a number in brackets after the first person singular (*I*-form) of the verb tells you which conjugation that verb belongs to.

So: neco (1) I kill   The (1) tells you that this verb behaves like *amo*.
      habeo (2) I have   The (2) tells you that this verb behaves like *moneo*.
      curro (3) I run   The (3) tells you that this verb behaves like *rego*.
      venio (4) I come   The (4) tells you that this verb behaves like *audio*.

From now on, more information will be given to you about each verb you come across. You will be given three pieces of information, then the conjugation number, then the English meaning. These are called the Principal Parts of the verb ('principal' means 'main'). If you know all this information about a Latin verb you will be able to work out all the different parts of it. Here are some examples:

amo, amare, amavi (1)	*I like*
moneo, monere, monui (2)	*I warn*
rego, regere, rexi (3)	*I rule*
audio, audire, audivi (4)	*I hear*
sum, esse, fui (irreg.)	*I am*

Now the explanation of these three principal parts:

1st word: (will usually end on -*o*):	1st person singular, present tense.
2nd word: (will usually end in -*re*):	the infinitive, or *to*-word.
3rd word: (will end in -*i*):	1st person singular, perfect tense.

So, the third principal part, ending in -*i*, is the start of the perfect tense.

If you remove this final -*i* you are left with the perfect stem, onto which you can add the six perfect personal endings:

-i	*I*
-isti	*you* (sg)
-it	*he/she/it*
-imus	*we*
-istis	*you* (pl)
-erunt	*they*

The exercises on the next page are based on the principal parts of these verbs:

I am	sum, esse, **fui** (irreg.)
I capture	capio, capere, **cepi** (3½)
I fight	pugno, pugnare, **pugnavi** (1)
I give	do, dare, **dedi** (1)
I hear	audio, audire, **audivi** (4)
I lead	duco, ducere, **duxi** (3)
I like	amo, amare, **amavi** (1)
I remain	maneo, manere, **mansi** (2)
I rule	rego, regere, **rexi** (3)
I run	curro, currere, **cucurri** (3)
I send	mitto, mittere, **misi** (3)
I warn	moneo, monere, **monui** (2)

Reminder

The third principal part, ending in **-i**, starts off that verb's perfect tense.

Take away that final **-i** and you are left with the perfect stem: this is what you add each of the six personal endings on to!

Exercise 34.1

Translate into Latin:

1. I ran. ....

2. You (sg) captured. ....

3. She led. ....

4. You (pl) ruled. ....

5. He gave. ....

6. They remained. ....

7. We ran. ....

8. He warned. ....

9. We sent. ....

10. They were. ....

Exercise 34.2

Translate into Latin:

1. We gave. ....

2. We led. ....

3. He ran. ....

4. You (sg) warned. ....

5. He was. ....

6. He remained. ....

7. They ran. ....

8. You (pl) gave. ....

9. They fought. ....

10. She ruled. ....

Handy Help

Perfect tenses in bold		Personal endings	
I am	sum, esse, **fui** (irreg.)	**-i**	I
I capture	capio, capere, **cepi** (3½)	**-isti**	you (sg)
I fight	pugno, pugnare, **pugnavi** (1)	**-it**	he/she/it
I give	do, dare, **dedi** (1)	**-imus**	we
I hear	audio, audire, **audivi** (4)	**-istis**	you (pl)
I lead	duco, ducere, **duxi** (3)	**-erunt**	they
I like	amo, amare, **amavi** (1)		
I remain	maneo, manere, **mansi** (2)		
I rule	rego, regere, **rexi** (3)		
I run	curro, currere, **cucurri** (3)		
I send	mitto, mittere, **misi** (3)		
I warn	moneo, monere, **monui** (2)		

Exercise 34.3

Translate into English:

1. equus bene cucurrit.

   ....

2. servi diu manserunt.

   ....

3. regina bene rexit.

   ....

4. pueri boni fuerunt.

   ....

5. maritus pecuniam misit.

   ....

6. nautae reginam amaverunt.

   ....

7. dominus servos monuit.

   ....

8. Graeci Troiam ceperunt.

   ....

9. ancilla pericula amavit.

   ....

10. incolae terram rexerunt.

    ....

Handy Help

Perfect tenses in bold		Personal endings	
I am	sum, esse, **fui** (irreg.)	**-i**	I
I capture	capio, capere, **cepi** (3½)	**-isti**	you (sg)
I fight	pugno, pugnare, **pugnavi** (1)	**-it**	he/she/it
I give	do, dare, **dedi** (1)	**-imus**	we
I hear	audio, audire, **audivi** (4)	**-istis**	you (pl)
I lead	duco, ducere, **duxi** (3)	**-erunt**	they
I like	amo, amare, **amavi** (1)		
I remain	maneo, manere, **mansi** (2)		
I rule	rego, regere, **rexi** (3)		
I run	curro, currere, **cucurri** (3)		
I send	mitto, mittere, **misi** (3)		
I warn	moneo, monere, **monui** (2)		

Exercise 34.4

Translate into Latin:

1. The horses remained there.

   ....

2. The slaves fought well.

   ....

3. The queen never ruled well.

   ....

4. The shields were big.

   ....

5. The sailor sent food.

   ....

6. The slave liked the master

   ....

7. The master liked the letter.

   ....

8. The slaves led the horses.

   ....

9. The friends heard the words.

   ....

10. The queen captured the island.

    ....

Handy Help

Perfect tenses in bold		Personal endings	
I am	sum, esse, **fui** (irreg.)	**-i**	I
I capture	capio, capere, **cepi** (3½)	**-isti**	you (sg)
I fight	pugno, pugnare, **pugnavi** (1)	**-it**	he/she/it
I give	do, dare, **dedi** (1)	**-imus**	we
I hear	audio, audire, **audivi** (4)	**-istis**	you (pl)
I lead	duco, ducere, **duxi** (3)	**-erunt**	they
I like	amo, amare, **amavi** (1)		
I remain	maneo, manere, **mansi** (2)		
I rule	rego, regere, **rexi** (3)		
I run	curro, currere, **cucurri** (3)		
I send	mitto, mittere, **misi** (3)		
I warn	moneo, monere, **monui** (2)		

Exercise 34.5

Translate into English:

1. puellae in horto diu manserunt.

   ....

2. dominus pecuniam servis dedit.

   ....

3. femina pueros de periculis monuit.

   ....

4. equi domini in agros cucurrerunt.

   ....

5. servi vinum ad dominum miserunt.

   ....

6. nauta equum ex agro duxit.

   ....

7. multae ancillae pecuniam domino bono dederunt.

   ....

8. servus domini iratus et malus fuit.

   ....

9. socii multos captivos in saevo proelio ceperunt.

   ....

10. parvus puer ex magno templo deorum cucurrit.

    ....

Handy Help

Principal parts of verbs used in this exercise (perfect tenses in bold)		Personal endings	
capio, capere, **cepi** (3½)	I take, capture	**-i**	I
curro, currere, **cucurri** (3)	I run	**-isti**	you (sg)
do, dare, **dedi** (1)	I give	**-it**	he/she/it
duco, ducere, **duxi** (3)	I lead	**-imus**	we
maneo, manere, **mansi** (2)	I stay, remain	**-istis**	you (pl)
mitto, mittere, **misi** (3)	I send	**-erunt**	they
moneo, monere, **monui** (2)	I warn		
sum, esse, **fui** (irreg.)	I am		

Chapter 35
Romulus and Remus: Part 8

Exercise 35.1
Translate into English.

Romulus and Remus argue about the signs from the gods.

1 Romulus <u>haec</u> verba Remo <u>dixit</u>: 'Reme, <u>aquilasne</u> vidisti?

ego <u>duodecim</u> <u>aquilas</u> vidi. tu <u>modo</u> sex vidisti. in <u>hoc</u> loco

igitur oppidum nostrum novum <u>aedificabo</u>. <u>hic</u> locus <u>sacer</u>

est.' Remus, ubi verba Romuli audivit, iratus erat. Romulo

5 respondit: 'es<u>ne</u> <u>insanus</u>, Romule? ego sex <u>aquilas</u> <u>meas</u>

vidi <u>antequam</u> tu <u>duodecim</u> <u>aquilas</u> <u>tuas</u> vidisti. ego igitur,

non tu, oppidum novum <u>aedificabo</u>.' pueri non laeti erant.

itaque Romulus et Remus et socii inter <u>se</u> <u>disputabant</u>.

haec = these
dico, -ere, dixi (3) = I say
aquila = eagle
-ne = *turns the sentence into a question*
duodecim = twelve
modo = only
hoc = this
aedificabo = I shall build
hic = this
sacer = sacred
insanus, -a, -um = mad
meus, -a, -um = my
antequam = before
tuus, -a, -um = your

se = themselves
disputo (1) = I argue

(A copy of this passage in workbook format can be found on page 117.)

Exercise 35.2
Answer these questions. They are based on the passage above. Complete English sentences are not required.

1. From the passage, give, in Latin, one example of each of the following:
   a. a neuter noun;
   b. a cardinal number;
   c. an adjective.

2. **Remo** (line 1). In what case is this noun?

3. **vidisti** (line 2). Give the tense of this verb.

4. **audivit** (line 4). Give the Latin subject and the Latin object of this verb.

5. **erat** (line 4). Give the first person singular of the present tense of this verb.

6. **vidi** (line 6). Give the person and number of this verb.

Vocabulary Box 24a	
dico, dicere, dixi (3)	I say, tell
meus, mea, meum	my
-ne	*(question suffix – see next page)*
sacer, sacra, sacrum	sacred
tuus, tua, tuum	your (sg)

Vocabulary Box 24b	
my	meus, mea, meum
sacred	sacer, sacra, sacrum
I say, tell	dico, dicere, dixi (3)
your (sg)	tuus, tua, tuum
question?	-ne *(see next page)*

Chapter 36
Questions using -ne

In the last reading passage we came across these sentences:

Reme, aquila**ne** vidisti?	*Remus, did you see the eagles?*
es**ne** insanus, Romule?	*Are you mad, Romulus?*

The **ne** stuck on to the end of the words aquilas and esne is one way of asking a simple question in Latin. It is expecting a simple answer, either a yes or a no.

In English, a statement is often turned into this sort of question by altering the word order and adding a question mark at the end.

Examples

Statement	**Question**
He is walking.	Is he walking?
We were laughing.	Were we laughing?
They saw.	Did they see?

In Latin, to change a statement into an open question you do two simple things:
1. Add **-ne** to the end of the **first** word in the Latin sentence.
2. Add a question mark at the end of the sentence.

Examples

Statement	**Question**
ambulat.	ambulat**ne**?
He is walking.	*Is he walking?*
puellae ridebant.	puellae**ne** ridebant**?**
The girls were laughing.	*Were the girls laughing?*
Romulus aquilam vidit.	Romulus**ne** aquilam vidit?
Romulus saw an eagle.	*Did Romulus see an eagle?*

If you are a grammar nerd you may be interested to know that the technical term for **-ne** is an enclitic interrogative particle. Enclitic means leaning closely upon the word in front; interrogative means asking a question; and particle just means something small. This sort of **ne** will usually be printed with a dash in front of it, **-ne,** because it does not exist as a word on its own; it is always stuck on the end of another word.

Vocabulary Box 25a	
consumo, -ere, consumpsi (3)	I eat
ludo, -ere, lusi (3)	I play
ostendo, -ere, ostendi (3)	I show

Vocabulary Box 25b	
I eat	consumo, -ere, consumpsi (3)
I play	ludo, -ere, lusi (3)
I show	ostendo, -ere, ostendi (3)

Exercise 36.1

Translate into Latin:

1. ridentne?
2. cantatne?
3. oppugnamusne?
4. ludisne?
5. scribebatne?
6. dormiebantne?
7. navigabamusne?
8. vidistine?
9. pugnaveruntne?
10. mansitne?

Exercise 36.2

Translate into Latin:

1. Are the girls laughing?
2. Is the master sleeping?
3. Were the slaves playing?
4. Was the friend coming?
5. Did the men depart?
6. Was the son listening?
7. Did the boy laugh?
8. Were the freedmen afraid?
9. Did the farmers attack?
10. Is the daughter drinking?

Exercise 36.3

Translate into English:

1. puerne puellam amat?
2. magisterne cibum consumpsit?
3. servine vinum bibebant?
4. incolaene templum aedificaverunt?
5. virine scuta portabant?

Exercise 36.4

Translate into Latin:

1. Do girls always like boys?
2. Did the farmer lead the horses into the field?
3. Were the slave girls playing in the garden?
4. Did the farmers stay in the field for a long time?
5. Was the master showing the money to the slaves?

Chapter 37
Romulus and Remus: Part 9

Exercise 37.1
Translate into English.

An argument has deadly results.

1 Romulus et Remus <u>disputabant</u>. Remus et socii suum oppidum

novum in <u>monte Aventino</u> aedificare constituerunt. in <u>monte</u>

<u>Palatio</u> Romulus et socii muros suos aedificare constituerunt.

olim Remus oppidum Romuli <u>visitavit</u>.

5 Romulus muros oppidi sui Remo ostendit. Remus, ubi muros

Romuli spectavit, risit. ad Romulum <u>etiam</u> cucurrit et clamavit:

'tui muri parvi, non <u>validi</u> sunt. numquam oppidum tuum bene

<u>protegent</u>! <u>quis</u> <u>hos</u> aedificavit?'

<u>saevus</u> Romulus, ubi verba Remi audivit, magnopere iratus

10 erat. gladium subito cepit, ad Remum cucurrit, <u>eum</u> gladio

necavit.

disputo (1) = I argue

monte Aventino = the Aventine Hill

monte Palatio = the Palatine Hill

visito (1) = I visit

etiam = even

validus = strong
protegent = (they) will protect
quis? = who?
hos = these

saevus = savage

eum = him

(A copy of this passage in workbook format can be found on page 118.)

Exercise 37.2
Answer these questions. They are based on the passage above. Complete English sentences are not required.

1. From the passage, give, in Latin, one example of each of the following:
    a. an adjective;
    b. a part of the verb *to be*;
    c. an adverb.

2. **aedificare** (line 2). What name is given to this part of the verb?

3. **visitavit** (line 4). Give the Latin subject and the Latin object of this verb.

4. **muros** (line 5). In which case is this noun? Why is this case used?

5. **cepit** (line 10). Give the first person singular of the present tense of this verb.

6. **gladio** (line 11). Give the case of this noun.

Vocabulary Box 26a	
etiam	also, even
quis?	who?
saevus, -a, -um	savage
validus, -a, -um	strong

Vocabulary Box 26b	
also, even	etiam
savage	saevus, -a, -um
strong	validus, -a, -um
who?	quis?

Chapter 38
Compound verbs

You have already met the verb 'to be' – *sum*. Two other verbs behave just like it, but with the additon of a prefix (a bit stuck on the front) at the beginning. These form a trio, and often cause problems because the prefix is not appreciated, so study these carefully:

sum (*I am*)   esse (*to be*)   fui (*I was*)
adsum (*I am present*)   **ad**esse (*to be present*)   **ad**fui (*I was present*)
absum (*I am away*)   **ab**esse (*to be away*)   **a**fui (*I was away*)

	sum, esse, fui *I am*	adsum, adesse, adfui *I am present*	absum, abesse, afui *I am away/absent*
Present	sum	adsum	absum
	es	ades	abes
	est	adest	abest
	sumus	adsumus	absumus
	estis	adestis	abestis
	sunt	adsunt	absunt
Imperfect	eram	aderam	abcram
	eras	aderas	aberas
	erat	aderat	aberat
	eramus	aderamus	aberamus
	eratis	aderatis	aberatis
	erant	aderant	aberant
Perfect	fui	adfui	afui
	fuisti	adfuisti	afuisti
	fuit	adfuit	afuit
	fuimus	adfuimus	afuimus
	fuistis	adfuistis	afuistis
	fuerunt	adfuerunt	afuerunt

adsum and *absum* are called 'compound verbs', because they are compounded (put together, from the Latin *cum*, 'with' and *pono*, 'I put') of the base verb with a prefix added. You will come across several of these as you study more Latin. For example:

base verb: porto – *I carry*

compounds: exporto – I *carry out*
            importo – *I carry in*
            transporto – *I carry across*

Exercise 38.1

Translate into English:

1. ubi sunt pueri? absunt.

   ....

2. ubi magister abest, pueri et puellae ludere amant.

   ....

3. servi non laborabant quod dominus aberat.

   ....

4. multi viri in oppido aderant.

   ....

5. cur aberas, puer? aberam quod laborare non cupiebam.

   ....

6. vir feminae diu afuit.

   ....

7. servus semper bene laborat ubi dominus adest.

   ....

8. cur in villa non aderatis, ancillae?

   ....

9. in villa non aderamus quod in agris laborabamus.

   ....

10. multi agricolae in agris semper adsunt.

    ....

Exercise 38.2

Translate into Latin:

1. Many friends were present in the villa.

   ....

2. Because the teacher was away, the boys were not working.

   ....

3. Friend, why were you not present in the forum?

   ....

4. I was not present in the forum because I was not in town.

   ....

5. The girls have often been away.

   ....

Exercise 22.1 (page 66)

Translate the following passage into good English.

Amulius' slaves carry out his cruel orders.

1 Amulius, ubi Romulum et Remum videt, <u>iratus</u> est. pueros

<u>parvos</u> statim necare constituit. Amulius <u>igitur</u> servos vocat.

servos pueros <u>capere</u> iubet. servos pueros ad <u>fluvium</u>

portare iubet. servos pueros in aquam <u>iacere</u> iubet. servi

5 <u>tamen</u>, quod pueros amant, <u>hoc</u> <u>facere</u> non cupiunt. sed

Amulium timent. Amulium magnopere timent. pueros <u>igitur</u>

<u>capiunt</u>, <u>eos</u> ad <u>fluvium</u> portant, <u>eos</u> in aquam <u>iaciunt</u>.

<u>deinde</u> discedunt.

iratus = angry

parvos = little
igitur = therefore

capio (3½) = I take, capture
fluvius = river
iacio (3½) = I throw

tamen = however
hoc = this (acusative)
facio (3½) = I do, make

eos = themselves

deinde = then, next

....

....

....

....

....

....

....

....

....

....

....

....

....

....

....

....

Exercise 25.1 (page 74)
Translate into English.

Romulus and Remus are saved by the gods.

1 Romulus et Remus in <u>fluvio</u> iam sunt. aquam
magnopere timent. aqua pueros per <u>fluvium</u> portat. in
<u>magno</u> periculo sunt. dei tamen, ubi <u>parvos</u> pueros in
<u>fluvio</u> vident, <u>eos</u> <u>servare</u> constituunt. undae pueros ad

5 terram <u>mox</u> portant et <u>ibi</u> <u>ponunt</u>. pueri, quod <u>fessi</u>
sunt, in terra dormiunt. <u>ibi</u> diu <u>manent</u>. <u>itaque</u> Romulus
et Remus iam <u>tuti</u> sunt.

fluvius = river

magnus = great, big
parvos = small, little
eos = them
servo (1) = I save
mox = soon
ibi = there
pono (3) = I put
fessi = tired
maneo (2) = I stay, re-
main
itaque = and so
tuti = safe

....
....
....
....
....
....
....
....
....
....
....
....
....
....
....
....
....
....

Exercise 27.1 (page 79)
Translate into English.

Romulus and Remus are helped by a she-wolf and a woodpecker.

1 Romulus et Remus in terra sunt. pueri aquam bibunt, sed

cibum non habent. in magno periculo igitur <u>adhuc</u> sunt.

prope <u>fluvium</u> habitat <u>lupa</u>. <u>lupa</u>, ubi prope <u>fluvium</u>

ambulat, <u>subito</u> <u>duos</u> pueros parvos videt. <u>eos</u> <u>servare</u>

5 constituit. Romulum et Remum <u>domum</u> portat. <u>lupa</u>

amicum bonum habet. amicus <u>lupae</u> est <u>picus</u>. <u>lupa</u> et

<u>picus</u> pueros diu <u>curant</u>. <u>lupa</u> <u>lac</u>, <u>picus</u> cibum Romulo et

Remo dat. pueri iam tuti et laeti sunt.

adhuc = still
fluvius = river
lupa = she-wolf
subito = suddenly
duos = two
eos = them
servo (1) = I save
domum = (to) home
picus = woodpecker
curo (1) = I look after
lac = milk

....

....

....

....

....

....

....

....

....

....

....

....

....

....

....

....

....

....

Exercise 29.1 (page 85)
Translate into English.

Faustulus, a shepherd, finds Romulus and Remus.

1 Romulus et Remus cum lupa et pico diu manserunt. olim
pastor, Faustulus, parvos pueros in agris conspexit. ubi eos
vidit, attonitus erat. ad villam suam cucurrit. hic habitabat
Faustulus cum uxore, Acca. Accae clamavit: 'Acca, veni

5 statim! curre!' Acca Faustulo respondit: 'quid est, Faustule?
cur clamas? responde!' Faustulus Accae respondit: 'duos
parvos pueros inveni. in periculo sunt.' Acca Faustulo respondit: 'ubi sunt, Faustule?' Faustulus iterum clamavit: 'in
agris sunt. veni! festina!' itaque Faustulus et Acca ad agros

10 statim festinaverunt. ibi Romulum et Remum invenerunt et
ad villam duxerunt.

lupa = wolf
picus = woodpecker
manserunt = (they) stayed
olim = one day
pastor = shepherd
conspexit = (he) caught sight of
eos = them
attonitus = amazed
suus = his
cucurrit = he ran
hic = here
uxore = wife
clamavit = he shouted
respondit = (she/he) replied
quid? = what?
inveni = I have found
ubi? = where?
iterum = again
festinaverunt = (they hurried)
invenerunt = they found
duxerunt = they led

....

....

....

....

....

....

....

....

....

....

....

....

....

....

....

....

Exercise 31.1 (page 89)
Translate into English.

Romulus and Remus grow up but eventually decide to leave Acca and Faustulus.

1   Romulus et Remus tuti iam erant. in villa Accae et

Faustuli diu habitaverunt. mox parvi pueri iuvenes

habitaverunt = they lived
iuvenes = young men
tandem = at last, finally
novus = new
cupiverunt = they wanted

erant. tandem, quod suum oppidum novum

aedificare cupiverunt, a villa discedere

5   constituerunt. ad Accam et Faustulum igitur

constituerunt = they decided

appropinquaverunt et haec verba dixerunt:

'Acca et Faustule, nos vos magnopere amamus.

appropinquaverunt = they approached
haec = these
dixerunt = (they) said
nos = we
vos = you (accusative)

sed discedere et novum oppidum aedificare

cupimus. oppidum nostrum magnum et pulchrum

10 et notum erit.'

noster = our
pulcher = beautiful
notus = well known
erit = (it) will be

....

....

....

....

....

....

....

....

....

....

....

....

....

....

....

Exercise 33.1 (page 93)
Translate into English.

The gods give Romulus and Remus some guidance.

1 Romulus et Remus et amici ad <u>fluvium</u> <u>venerunt</u>.

<u>nomen</u> <u>fluvii</u> erat <u>Tiberis</u>. pueri et amici suum oppidum

novum in <u>hoc</u> loco aedificare <u>constituerunt</u>. prope <u>fluvium</u>

erat septem <u>colles</u>. Romulus <u>primum</u> <u>collem</u>, Remus

5 <u>secundum</u> <u>collem</u> <u>ascendit</u>. pueri iam fessi erant. hic

<u>steterunt</u> et <u>signum</u> deorum <u>exspectaverunt</u>. non diu

<u>exspectaverunt</u>. Remus sex <u>aquilas</u> in caelo <u>conspexit</u>.

ubi <u>aquilas</u> <u>vidit</u>, laetus erat. <u>risit</u>. deinde Romulus

<u>duodecim</u> <u>aquilas</u> in caelo <u>conspexit</u>. ubi <u>aquilas</u> <u>vidit</u>,

10 laetus erat. <u>risit</u>.

fluvius, -i m. = river
venerunt = (they) came
nomen = name
Tiberis = the Tiber
hoc = this
constituerunt = (they) decided
colles = hills
primus, -a, -um = first
collem = hill

secundus, -a, -um = second
ascendit = (he) climbed
steterunt = they stood
signum, -i n. = signal
exspectaverunt = they waited for
aquila, -ae f. = eagle
conspexit = (he) caught sight of
vidit = he saw
risit = he laughed
duodecim = twelve

....
....
....
....
....
....
....
....
....
....
....
....
....
....

Exercise 35.1 (page 101)
Translate into English.

Romulus and Remus argue about the signs from the gods.

1 Romulus <u>haec</u> verba Remo <u>dixit</u>: 'Reme, <u>aquilasne</u> vidisti?

ego <u>duodecim</u> <u>aquilas</u> vidi. tu <u>modo</u> sex vidisti. in <u>hoc</u> loco

igitur oppidum nostrum novum <u>aedificabo</u>. <u>hic</u> locus <u>sacer</u>

est.' Remus, ubi verba Romuli audivit, iratus erat. Romulo

5 respondit: 'es<u>ne</u> <u>insanus</u>, Romule? ego sex <u>aquilas</u> <u>meas</u>

vidi <u>antequam</u> tu <u>duodecim</u> <u>aquilas</u> <u>tuas</u> vidisti. ego igitur,

non tu, oppidum novum <u>aedificabo</u>.' pueri non laeti erant.

itaque Romulus et Remus et socii inter <u>se</u> <u>disputabant</u>.

haec = these
dico, -ere, dixi (3) = I say
aquila = eagle
-ne = *turns the sentence into a question*
duodecim = twelve
modo = only
hoc = this
aedificabo = I shall build
hic = this
sacer = sacred
insanus, -a, -um = mad
meus, -a, -um = my
antequam = before
tuus, -a, -um = your

se = themselves
disputo (1) = I argue

....

....

....

....

....

....

....

....

....

....

....

....

....

....

....

....

Exercise 37.1 (page 104)
Translate into English.

An argument has deadly results.

1   Romulus et Remus <u>disputabant</u>. Remus et socii suum

oppidum novum in <u>monte Aventino</u> aedificare constituerunt.

in <u>monte Palatio</u> Romulus et socii muros suos aedificare

constituerunt. olim Remus oppidum Romuli <u>visitavit</u>.

5   Romulus muros oppidi sui Remo ostendit. Remus, ubi muros

Romuli spectavit, risit. ad Romulum <u>etiam</u> cucurrit et

clamavit: 'tui muri parvi, non <u>validi</u> sunt. numquam oppidum

tuum bene <u>protegent</u>! <u>quis</u> <u>hos</u> aedificavit?'

<u>saevus</u> Romulus, ubi verba Remi audivit, magnopere iratus

10 erat. gladium subito cepit, ad Remum cucurrit, <u>eum</u> gladio

necavit.

disputo (1) = I argue

monte Aventino = the Aventine Hill

monte Palatio = the Palatine Hill

visito (1) = I visit

etiam = even

validus = strong
protegent = (they) will protect
quis? = who?
hos = these

saevus = savage

eum = him

....

....

....

....

....

....

....

....

....

....

....

....

....

....

English into Latin Practice Tests

The vocabulary of these tests is limited to the wordlist prescribed by the ISEB syllabus. If you know your grammar, and have learned by heart the priority English-Latin vocabulary items marked with an ! in the Vocabulary Boxes, you should be able to tackle these without looking anything up. Good luck!

Test 1 after Chapter 9

1. We love the queen.
2. Spears kill.
3. We do not often kill slaves.
4. I do not have a villa.
5. I fear the queen.

Test 2 after Chapter 11

1. She has a villa and money.
2. The girl is not a queen.
3. We are building a road.
4. The maidservant is preparing dinner.
5. The sailors are always shouting.

Test 3 after Chapter 16

1. You (sg) see the letter.
2. The master does not fear slaves.
3. We are destroying the villa.
4. Women do not build walls.
5. Slaves do not often have money.

Test 4 after Chapter 17

1. The slaves are building a road.
2. Queens fear the gods.
3. The master is killing a slave.
4. I like the woman and (her) son.
5. The queen fears the gods.

Test 5 after Chapter 19

1. Sailors like books.
2. Boys are always shouting.
3. We like books.
4. We have swords.
5. Boys do not often carry spears.

Test 6 after Chapter 21

1. The slaves are preparing dinner.
2. Masters have villas and slaves.
3. The slaves are building a road.
4. They are boys.
5. The man is building a wall.

Test 7 after Chapter 23

1. The slave likes the book.
2. The girls fear the teacher.
3. Gods like temples.
4. The man sees the girl.
5. The queen is entering the temple.

Test 8 after Chapter 25

1. We like towns and villas.
2. The son likes wine.
3. We love the gods.
4. Boys do not often like books.
5. She is not the queen.

Test 9 after Chapter 27

1. We fear the gods.
2. Teachers do not kill boys.
3. We like books and letters.
4. They are Romans.
5. We often look at horses.

Test 10 after Chapter 29

1. The slave girl was preparing dinner.
2. The teacher always carries books.
3. The girls were often shouting.
4. The master has a villa and horses.
5. The teacher was praising the boys.

Test 11 after Chapter 31

1. The master was warning the slave girl.
2. The man was looking at the woman.
3. The slave girls do not like the master.
4. He does not have a friend.
5. The Romans used to build roads and towns.

Test 12 after Chapter 33

1. The slaves were building temples.
2. The sailor has a sword and a spear.
3. The master was praising the dinner.
4. The girl was afraid of the sailor.
5. You (sg) are not entering the town.

Test 13 after Chapter 35

1. The slave was carrying money.
2. The friend has a spear and a sword.
3. They were looking at the temples.
4. The horse is carrying a man.
5. The boys and girls were watching the queen.

Test 14 after Chapter 37

1. Teachers do not often have friends.
2. The gods were warning the Romans.
3. The men were sailors.
4. The boy was praising the book.
5. The queen has a letter.

Test 15

1. Teachers often warn.
2. We were looking at the money.
3. The Romans were carrying swords.
4. The boys like the teacher.
5. The slaves were building a wall.

Test 16

1. The son likes the wine and the dinner.
2. The Romans were destroying the wall.
3. The master was calling the horses.
4. The slave was afraid of the master.
5. The sailor was carrying money.

Test 17

1. The Romans used to like wines.
2. We often look at temples.
3. The slaves feared the master.
4. We are not maidservants.
5. The men and women were shouting.

Test 18

1. The man was praising the gods.
2. We were building a town.
3. The teacher was praising the boys and girls.
4. The Romans were destroying the towns.
5. The slaves are building villas.

Reference Section

List 1: Vocabulary Checklist

		...leep
		...right, famous
	angry	
7.	laetus	happy
8.	magnus	big, great
9.	malus	bad, evil, wicked
10.	meus	my
11.	miser	miserable
12.	multus	much, many
13.	noster	our
14.	notus	well known
15.	novus	new
16.	parvus	small
17.	pulcher	beautiful, handsome
18.	Romanus	Roman
19.	sacer	sacred
20.	saevus	savage
21.	suus	his/her/their own
22.	Troianus	Trojan
23.	tutus	safe
24.	tuus	your (sg)
25.	validus	strong
26.	vester	your (pl)

Adverbs

27.	bene	well
28.	diu	for a long time
29.	fortiter	bravely
30.	hic	here
31.	iam	now, already
32.	ibi	there
33.	iterum	again
34.	magnopere	greatly
35.	mox	soon
36.	non	not
37.	numquam	never
38.	olim	one day, once upon a time
39.	saepe	often
40.	semper	always
41.	sic	in this way, thus
42.	statim	immediately
43.	subito	suddenly
44.	tandem	finally

Conjunctions

45.	deinde	then, next
46.	et	and
47.	etiam	also, even
48.	igitur	therefore
49.	itaque	and so
50.	quod	because
51.	sed	but
52.	tamen	however
53.	ubi	when

Interrogatives (question words)

54.	cur?	why?
55.	-ne	(indicates a question)
56.	quid?	what?
57.	quis?	who?
58.	ubi?	where?

Nouns

59.	ancilla	slave girl, maidservant
60.	aqua	water
61.	cena	dinner
62.	dea	goddess
63.	domina	mistress
64.	epistula	letter
65.	femina	woman
66.	filia	daughter
67.	Graecia	Greece
68.	hasta	spear
69.	insula	island
70.	ira	anger
71.	patria	homeland
72.	pecunia	money
73.	puella	girl
74.	regina	queen
75.	Roma	Rome
76.	sagitta	arrow
77.	silva	wood
78.	terra	land
79.	Troia	Troy
80.	turba	crowd
81.	unda	wave
82.	via	road
83.	villa	villa
84.	agricola	farmer
85.	incola	inhabitant
86.	nauta	sailor
87.	poeta	poet
88.	ager	field
89.	amicus	friend
90.	captivus	prisoner
91.	cibus	food
92.	deus	god
93.	dominus	master

94.	equus	horse	139.	per + acc	through, along
95.	filius	son	140.	prope + acc	near
96.	gladius	sword	141.	trans + acc	across
97.	hortus	garden			
98.	liber	book	142.	in + abl	in, on
99.	libertus	freedman, ex-slave	143.	in + acc	into
100.	locus	place			

Pronouns

101.	magister	teacher, master
102.	maritus	husband
103.	murus	wall
104.	nuntius	messenger
105.	puer	boy
106.	servus	slave
107.	socius	ally
108.	ventus	wind
109.	vir	man
110.	aurum	gold
111.	auxilium	help
112.	bellum	war
113.	caelum	sky
114.	consilium	plan
115.	forum	forum, market place
116.	oppidum	town
117.	periculum	danger
118.	proelium	battle
119.	scutum	shield
120.	templum	temple
121.	verbum	word
122.	vinum	wine

Pronouns

144.	ego	I
145.	nos	we
146.	tu	you (sg)
147.	vos	you (pl)

Verbs (1)

148.	aedifico	build
149.	ambulo	walk
150.	amo	love, like
151.	canto	sing
152.	clamo	shout
153.	do	give
154.	festino	hurry
155.	habito	live
156.	intro	enter
157.	laboro	work
158.	laudo	praise
159.	navigo	sail
160.	neco	kill
161.	oppugno	attack
162.	paro	prepare
163.	porto	carry
164.	pugno	fight
165.	rogo	ask, ask for
166.	specto	watch, look at
167.	sto	stand
168.	supero	overcome
169.	voco	call

Numbers

123.	unus	one
124.	duo	two
125.	tres	three
126.	quattuor	four
127.	quinque	five
128.	sex	six
129.	septem	seven
130.	octo	eight
131.	novem	nine
132.	decem	ten

Verbs (2)

170.	deleo	destroy
171.	habeo	have
172.	iubeo	order
173.	maneo	stay
174.	moneo	warn
175.	moveo	move
176.	respondeo	reply
177.	rideo	laugh
178.	teneo	hold
179.	terreo	frighten
180.	timeo	fear
181.	video	see

Prepositions

133.	a/ab + abl	away from
134.	cum + abl	with
135.	de + abl	down from, about
136.	e/ex + abl	out of
137.	ad + acc	to, towards
138.	contra + acc	against

Verbs (3)

182.	bibo	drink
183.	constituo	decide
184.	consumo	eat
185.	curro	run
186.	dico	say
187.	discedo	depart
188.	duco	lead
189.	lego	read; choose
190.	ludo	play
191.	mitto	send
192.	ostendo	show
193.	pono	put
194.	rego	rule
195.	scribo	write

Verbs (3½)

196.	capio	take, capture
197.	cupio	want
198.	facio	do, make
199.	iacio	throw

Verbs (4)

200.	audio	hear, listen to
201.	dormio	sleep
202.	venio	come

Verbs (irreg)

203.	absum	be away
204.	adsum	be present
205.	sum	be

List 2: Principal Parts Checklist

present tense	infinitive	perfect tense
e.g. I build	to build	I built/I have built

First Conjugation

148.	aedifico	aedificare	aedificavi	build
149.	ambulo	ambulare	ambulavi	walk
150.	amo	amare	amavi	love, like
151.	canto	cantare	cantavi	sing
152.	clamo	clamare	clamavi	shout
153.	do	dare	dedi	give
154.	festino	festinare	festinavi	hurry
155.	habito	habitare	habitavi	live
156.	intro	intrare	intravi	enter
157.	laboro	laborare	laboravi	work
158.	laudo	laudare	laudavi	praise
159.	navigo	navigare	navigavi	sail
160.	neco	necare	necavi	kill
161.	oppugno	oppugnare	oppugnavi	attack
162.	paro	parare	paravi	prepare
163.	porto	portare	portavi	carry
164.	pugno	pugnare	pugnavi	fight
165.	rogo	rogare	rogavi	ask, ask for
166.	specto	spectare	spectavi	watch, look at
167.	sto	stare	steti	stand
168.	supero	superare	superavi	overcome
169.	voco	vocare	vocavi	call

Second Conjugation

170. deleo	delere	delevi	destroy
171. habeo	habere	habui	have
172. iubeo	iubere	iussi	order
173. maneo	manere	mansi	stay
174. moneo	monere	monui	warn
175. moveo	movere	movi	move
176. respondeo	respondere	respondi	reply
177. rideo	ridere	risi	laugh
178. teneo	tenere	tenui	hold
179. terreo	terrere	terrui	frighten
180. timeo	timere	timui	fear
181. video	videre	vidi	see

Third Conjugation

182. bibo	bibere	bibi	drink
183. constituo	constituere	constitui	decide
184. consumo	consumere	consumpsi	eat
185. curro	currere	cucurri	run
186. dico	dicere	dixi	say
187. discedo	discedere	discessi	depart
188. duco	ducere	duxi	lead
189. lego	legere	legi	read; choose
190. ludo	ludere	lusi	play
191. mitto	mittere	misi	send
192. ostendo	ostendere	ostendi	show
193. pono	ponere	posui	put
194. rego	regere	rexi	rule
195. scribo	scribere	scripsi	write

Mixed Conjugation (3½)

196. capio	capere	cepi	take, capture
197. cupio	cupere	cupivi	want
198. facio	facere	feci	do, make
199. iacio	iacere	ieci	throw

Fourth Conjugation

200. audio	audire	audivi	hear, listen to
201. dormio	dormire	dormivi	sleep
202. venio	venire	veni	come

Irregulars

203. absum	abesse	afui	be away
204. adsum	adesse	adfui	be present
205. sum	esse	fui	be

List 3: English-into-Latin Sentences Revision

List 3a: Latin only Checklist

aedifico	filius	neco	servus
amicus	gladius	non	specto
amo	habeo	oppidum	sum
ancilla	hasta	paro	templum
cena	intro	pecunia	timeo
deleo	laudo	porto	via
deus	liber	puella	video
dominus	magister	puer	villa
epistula	moneo	regina	vinum
equus	mox	Romanus	vir
et	murus	saepe	voco
femina	nauta	semper	

List 3b: English – alphabetical checklist

and	et	not	non
be	sum	often	saepe
be afraid of	timeo	praise	laudo
book	liber	prepare	paro
boy	puer	queen	regina
build	aedifico	road	via
call	voco	Roman	Romanus
carry	porto	see	video
destroy	deleo	sailor	nauta
dinner	cena	slave	servus
enter	intro	slave-girl	ancilla
fear	timeo	son	filius
friend	amicus	soon	mox
girl	puella	spear	hasta
god	deus	street	via
have	habeo	sword	gladius
horse	equus	teacher	magister
kill	neco	temple	templum
letter	epistula	town	oppidum
like	amo	villa	villa
look at	specto	wall	murus
love	amo	warn	moneo
maidservant	ancilla	watch	specto
man	vir	wine	vinum
master	dominus, magister	woman	femina
meal	cena		

List 3c: English-Latin Nouns/Verbs/Others Checklist

Nouns

1.	book	liber
2.	boy	puer
3.	dinner	cena
4.	friend	amicus
5.	girl	puella
6.	god	deus
7.	horse	equus
8.	letter	epistula
9.	maidservant	ancilla
10.	man	vir
11.	master	dominus, magister
12.	meal	cena
13.	money	pecunia
14.	queen	regina
15.	road	via
16.	Roman	Roman
17.	sailor	nauta
18.	slave	servus
19.	slave-girl	ancilla
20.	son	filius
21.	spear	hasta
22.	street	via
23.	sword	gladius
24.	teacher	magister
25.	temple	templum
26.	town	oppidum
27.	villa	villa
28.	wall	murus
29.	wine	vinum
30.	woman	femina

Verbs

31.	be	sum
32.	build	aedifico
33.	call	voco
34.	carry	porto
35.	destroy	deleo
36.	enter	intro
37.	fear	timeo
38.	have	habeo
39.	kill	neco
40.	like	amo
41.	look at	specto
42.	love	amo
43.	praise	laudo
44.	prepare	paro
45.	see	video
46.	shout	clamo
47.	warn	moneo
48.	watch	specto

Others

49.	always	semper
50.	and	et
51.	not	non
52.	often	saepe

List 3d: English-Latin word groupings Checklist

Nouns

1. dinner — cena
2. girl — puella
3. letter — epistula
4. maidservant — ancilla
5. meal — cena
6. money — pecunia
7. queen — regina
8. road — via
9. nauta — sailor
10. slavegirl — ancilla
11. spear — hasta
12. street — via
13. villa — villa
14. woman — femina

15. friend — amicus
16. god — deus
17. horse — equus
18. master — dominus
19. Roman — Romanus
20. slave — servus
21. son — filius
22. sword — gladius
23. wall — murus

24. book — liber
25. boy — puer
26. man — vir
27. master — magister
28. teacher — magister

29. temple — templum
30. town — oppidum
31. wine — vinum

Verbs

32. build — aedifico
33. call — voco
34. carry — porto
35. enter — intro
36. kill — neco
37. like — amo
38. look at — specto
39. love — amo
40. praise — laudo
41. prepare — paro
42. shout — clamo
43. watch — specto

44. destroy — deleo
45. fear — timeo
46. have — habeo
47. see — video
48. warn — moneo

49. be — sum

Others

50. always — semper
51. and — et
52. not — non
53. often — saepe

List 4: Grammar Reference

List 4a: Grammatical Terms

adjectives   These are words that describe nouns. e.g. *bonus* (good), *pulcher* (beautiful).

adverbs   These are words which describe verbs. e.g. *bene* (well), *statim* (immediately)

cardinal number   *unus* (one), *duo* (two), *tres* (three) etc.

case   nominative (subject), vocative (person spoken to), accusative (object), genitive (of), dative (to or for) or ablative (by, with, from).

conjugation   A family of verbs which behave in the same way. e.g. *amo* (1) is in the first conjugation; *audio* (4) is in the fourth conjugation.

conjunction   A joining word. e.g. *et* (and), sed (but).

declension   A family of nouns which behave in the same way. e.g. *puella* (girl) is in the first declension; *servus* (slave) is in the second declension.

gender   Whether a noun or adjective is masculine, feminine or neuter.

imperative   An order. e.g. *audi!* (listen!), *amate!* (love!).

infinitive   A to-word, the second principal part of a verb, usually ending in -*re* in Latin. e.g. *amare* (to love). But beware of *esse* (to be).

noun   A person, place or thing

number   Whether a noun or verb is SINGULAR or PLURAL.

person   1st person singular = I; 2nd person singular = You 3rd person singular = He, She, It; 1st person plural = We; 2nd person plural = You; 3rd person plural = They

prepositions   Little words like *cum* (with), *ad* (to, towards), *in* (in). In Latin, some prepositions are followed by accusative nouns, others by ablative nouns.

tense   This describes the time when something is happening. You will meet three tenses in Level 1: present (happening now), imperfect (continuous action in the past) or perfect (a single, one-off action in the past).

verb   A doing word.

job	*examples*
subject (doer) of verb	servus laborat. *The slave is working.*
with the verb *to be*	Marcus est servus. *Marcus is a slave.*

	job	*examples*
vocative	person spoken to	serve, quid facis? *Slave, what are you doing?*
accusative	object (receiver) of verb	servum laudo. *I am praising the slave.*
	after prepositions like *ad*	ad servum currit. *He is running towards the slave.*
genitive	'of'	dominus servi est malus. *The master of the slave is wicked.*
dative	'to', 'for'	pecuniam servo dat. *He gives money to the slave.*
ablative	'by', 'with', 'from'	puerum gladio necat. *He kills the boy with his sword.*
	after some prepositions; for instance, *cum*	cum servo pugnat. *He is fighting with the slave.*

4b.2 Summary of nouns

Declension:		1	2	2	2	2
Gender:		f.	m.	m.	m.	n.
		girl	*slave*	*boy*	*field*	*war*
SINGULAR						
nominative	(subject)	puella	servus	puer	ager	bellum
vocative	(spoken to)	puella	serve	puer	ager	bellum
accusative	(object)	puellam	servum	puerum	agrum	bellum
genitive	('of')	puellae	servi	pueri	agri	belli
dative	('to'/'for')	puellae	servo	puero	agro	bello
ablative	('by'/'with'/'from')	puella	servo	puero	agro	bello
PLURAL						
nominative	(subjects)	puellae	servi	pueri	agri	bella
vocative	(spoken to)	puellae	servi	pueri	agri	bella
accusative	(objects)	puellas	servos	pueros	agros	bella
genitive	('of')	puellarum	servorum	puerorum	agrorum	bellorum
dative	('to'/'for')	puellis	servis	pueris	agris	bellis
ablative	('by'/'with'/'from')	puellis	servis	pueris	agris	bellis

List 4c: Adjectives

4c.1 Adjectives in *-us*

e.g. bonus (*good*)

		masculine	feminine	neuter
SINGULAR				
nominative	(subject)	bonus	bona	bonum
vocative	(spoken to)	bone	bona	bonum
accusative	(object)	bonum	bonam	bonum
genitive	('of')	boni	bonae	boni
dative	('to'/'for')	bono	bonae	bono
ablative	('by'/'with'/'from')	bono	bona	bono
PLURAL				
nominative	(subjects)	boni	bonae	bona
vocative	(spoken to)	boni	bonae	bona
accusative	(objects)	bonos	bonas	bona
genitive	('of')	bonorum	bonarum	bonorum
dative	('to'/'for')	bonis	bonis	bonis
ablative	('by'/'with'/'from')	bonis	bonis	bonis

4c.2 Adjectives in -er *(keeping the e)*

e.g. miser *(miserable)*

		masculine	feminine	neuter
SINGULAR				
nominative	(subject)	miser	misera	miserum
vocative	(spoken to)	miser	misera	miserum
accusative	(object)	miserum	miseram	miserum
genitive	('of')	miseri	miserae	miseri
dative	('to'/'for')	misero	miserae	misero
ablative	('by'/'with'/'from')	misero	misera	misero
PLURAL				
nominative	(subjects)	miseri	miserae	misera
vocative	(spoken to)	miseri	miserae	misera
accusative	(objects)	miseros	miseras	misera
genitive	('of')	miserorum	miserarum	miserorum
dative	('to'/'for')	miseris	miseris	miseris
ablative	('by'/'with'/'from')	miseris	miseris	miseris

4c.3 Adjectives in -er *(dropping the e)*

e.g. pulcher *(beautiful)*

		masculine	feminine	neuter
SINGULAR				
nominative	(subject)	pulcher	pulchra	pulchrum
vocative	(spoken to)	pulcher	pulchra	pulchrum
accusative	(object)	pulchrum	pulchram	pulchrum
genitive	('of')	pulchri	pulchrae	pulchri
dative	('to'/'for')	pulchro	pulchrae	pulchro
ablative	('by'/'with'/'from')	pulchro	pulchra	pulchro
PLURAL				
nominative	(subjects)	pulchri	pulchrae	pulchra
vocative	(spoken to)	pulchri	pulchrae	pulchra
accusative	(objects)	pulchros	pulchras	pulchra
genitive	('of')	pulchrorum	pulchrarum	pulchrorum
dative	('to'/'for')	pulchris	pulchris	pulchris
ablative	('by'/'with'/'from')	pulchris	pulchris	pulchris

List 4d: Pronouns

4d.1 First Person Pronoun: ego (*I*)

	singular		plural	
nominative (subject)	ego	I	nos	we
accusative (object)	me	me	nos	us

4d.2 Second Person Pronoun: tu (*you*)

	singular		plural	
nominative (subjects)	tu	you	vos	you
accusative (objects)	te	you	vos	you
nominative (subjects)	tu	you	vos	you
accusative (objects)	te	you	vos	you

List 4e: Prepositions

4e.1 Prepositions followed by the accusative case

ad + accusative	to, towards	ad reginam ambulat
		He is walking towards the queen.
contra + accusative	against	contra nautam pugnat.
		He is fighting against the sailor.
per + accusative	through, along	per viam currit.
		He is running along the road.
prope + accusative	near	prope murum stat.
		He is standing near the wall.
trans + accusative	across	trans viam festinat.
		He hurries across the road.

4e.2 Prepositions followed by the ablative case

a/ab + ablative	(away) from	ab insula navigat.
		He sails away from the island.
cum + ablative	with	cum amico ludit.
		He is playing with a friend.
de + ablative	down from, about	de periculo monet.
		He warns about the danger.
e/ex + ablative	out of	ex oppido currit.
		He runs out of the town.

4e.3 The Preposition *in*

This frequently causes problems, because it can be followed by an ablative word (when it means *in* or *on*) as well as by an accusative word (when it means *into*).

Examples

in + ablative = *in*	equus in agro currit.
	The horse is running in the field.
in + accusative = *into*	equus in agrum currit.
	The horse is running into the field.

List 4f: Verbs

4f.1 Present tense (happening now: 'is'/'are')

		1 love	2 warn	3 rule	3½ take	4 hear
1st pers sg	I	amo	moneo	rego	capio	audio
2nd pers sg	you (sg)	amas	mones	regis	capis	audis
3rd pers sg	he/she/it	amat	monet	regit	capit	audit
1st pers pl	we	amamus	monemus	regimus	capimus	audimus
2nd pers pl	you (pl)	amatis	monetis	regitis	capitis	auditis
3rd pers pl	they	amant	monent	regunt	capiunt	audiunt

4f.2 Imperfect tense (continuous action in the past: 'was/were -ing'/'used to...'/'would...')

1st pers sg	I	amabam	monebam	regebam	capiebam	audiebam
2nd pers sg	you (sg)	amabas	monebas	regebas	capiebas	audiebas
3rd pers sg	he/she/it	amabat	monebat	regebat	capiebat	audiebat
1st pers pl	we	amabamus	monebamus	regebamus	capiebamus	audiebamus
2nd pers pl	you (pl)	amabatis	monebatis	regebatis	capiebatis	audiebamus
3rd pers pl	they	amabant	monebant	regebant	capiebant	audiebant

4f.3 Perfect tense (single completed action in the past)

1st pers sg	I	amavi	monui	rexi	cepi	audivi
2nd pers sg	you (sg)	amavisti	monuisti	rexisti	cepisti	audivisti
3rd pers sg	he/she/it	amavit	monuit	rexit	cepit	audivit
1st pers pl	we	amavimus	monuimus	reximus	cepimus	audivimus
2nd pers pl	you (pl)	amavistis	monuistis	rexistis	cepistis	audivistis
3rd pers pl	they	amaverunt	monuerunt	rexerunt	ceperunt	audiverunt

4f.4 Infinitive ('to' word)

	amare	monere	regere	capere	audire
	to love	*to warn*	*to rule*	*to take*	*to hear*

4f.5 Imperative (giving an order)

singular:	ama!	mone!	rege!	cape!	audi!
plural:	amate!	monete!	regite!	capite!	audite!
	love!	*warn!*	*rule!*	*take!*	*hear!*

4f.6 Irregular verb: *sum* (*I am*)

Present: sum	Imperfect: eram	Perfect: fui	Infinitive (*to be*): esse
es	eras	fuisti	
est	erat	fuit	
sumus	eramus	fuimus	
estis	eratis	fuistis	
sunt	erant	fuerunt	

Imperative singular (*be!*): es!/esto!   Imperative plural (*be!*): este!/estote!

List 4g: Syntax

4g.1 Adverbs
Adverbs do not change their form in Latin. They will usually be found just before the verb at the end of the sentence.

> servi <u>fortiter</u> pugnant.   *The slaves fight <u>bravely</u>.*
> pueri <u>semper</u> <u>bene</u> laborant.   *Boys <u>always</u> work <u>well</u>.*

4g.2 quod (= *because*) clauses
These are straightforward:

> puella nautam amabat quod pecuniam habebat.
> *The girl liked the sailor because he had money.*

> servi, quod dominum timebant, fugerunt.
> *Because the slaves were afraid of their master, they fled.*

4g.3 ubi (= *when*) clauses
These also are straighforward:

> ubi magistrum vidit, perterritus erat.
> *When he saw the teacher, he was frightened.*

> servi, ubi pericula viderunt, cucurrerunt.
> *When the slaves saw the dangers, they ran.*

4g.4 Direct Questions: *-ne*
A Latin statement can be changed into a question be adding *-ne* to the end of the first word of the sentence and adding a question mark to the end of the sentence.

> laborat.   He is working.
> laborat**ne**?   *Is he working?*

> est fessus.   He is tired.
> est**ne** fessus?   *Is he tired?*

> puer puellam spectat.   The boy is looking at the girl.
> puer**ne** puellam spectat?   *Is the boy looking at the girl?*

4g.5   Present infinitives
These are *to*-words. In Latin they usually end in *-re*. You will find them used with the verbs *prepare* (paro), *want* (cupio), *decide* (constituo) and *order* (iubeo). The infinitive usually comes just before the main verb at the end of the sentence.

> puella <u>cantare</u> parat.   *The girl prepares <u>to sing</u>.*
> pueri <u>ludere</u> cupiunt.   *The boys want <u>to play</u>.*
> servi <u>pugnare</u> constituerunt.   *The slaves decided <u>to fight</u>.*
> dominus servos <u>laborare</u> iussit.   *The master ordered the slaves <u>to work</u>.*

List 4g.6: Cardinal Numbers 1-10

unus	one
duo	two
tres	three
quattuor	four
quinque	five
sex	six
septem	seven
octo	eight
novem	nine
decem	ten

Latin CE Level 1 Revision Check-list

	topic	quick reminder	example	1st check			2nd check		
				☹	😐	☺	☹	😐	☺
nouns	1st declension	mostly f.	puella						
	2nd declension	m.	servus						
	2nd declension	m. (keeping the *e*)	puer						
	2nd declension	m. (dropping the *e*)	ager						
	2nd declension	n.	bellum						
verbs	present tense	is/are 1st conjugation	amo						
		2nd conjugation	moneo						
		3rd conjugation	rego						
		4th conjugation	audio						
		to be - irreg	sum						
verbs	imperfect tense	was/were –ing, used to... 1st	amabam						
		2nd conjugation	monebam						
		3rd conjugation	regebam						
		4th conjugation	audiebam						
		to be - irreg	eram						
verbs	perfect tense	single action in past 1st	amavi						
		2nd conjugation	monui						
		3rd conjugation	rexi						
		4th conjugation	audivi						
		to be - irreg	fui						
verbs	infinitives	*to*-words 1st	amare						
		2nd conjugation	monere						
		3rd conjugation	regere						
		4th conjugation	audire						
		to be - irreg	esse						
verbs	imperatives	commands 1st	ama, amate						
		2nd conjugation	mone, monete						
		3rd conjugation	rege, regite						
		4th conjugation	audi, audite						
		to be - irreg	es/esto, este/estote						
adjectives	-us	servus/puella/bellum endings	bonus						
	-er	keeping the *e*	miser						
	-er	dropping the *e*	pulcher						
pronouns	*I* and *you*	*ego* and *tu*	ego/nos, tu/vos						
numbers		1-10	unus - decem						
GRAMMAR	cases	*what do they mean?*	nominative						
			vocative						
			accusative						
			genitive						
			dative						
			ablative						
	persons	I/we	1st						
		you	2nd						
		he/she/it/they	3rd						
	number	singular							
		plural							
	questions	(on end of first word)	-ne ?						
+ vocabulary!									

137

List 5: English-Latin Quick Checklist

sg = singular   pl = plural   abl = ablative   acc = accusative

about	de + abl.		depart	discedo (3)
across	trans + acc.		destroy	deleo (2)
again	iterum		dinner	cena
against	contra + acc.		do	facio (3½)
ally	socius		down from	de + abl.
along	per + acc.		drink	bibo (3)
already	iam			
also	etiam		eat	consumo (3)
always	semper		eight	octo
am	sum (irreg.)		enter	intro (1)
am present	adsum (irreg.)		especially	magnopere
and	et		even	etiam
and so	itaque		evil	malus
anger	ira		ex-slave	libertus
angry	iratus			
answer	respondeo (2)		famous	clarus
arrow	sagitta		farmer	agricola
ask, ask for	rogo (1)		fear	timeo (2)
at last	tandem		field	ager
attack	oppugno (1)		fight	pugno
away from	a/ab + abl.		finally	tandem
			five	quinque
bad	malus		food	cibus
battle	proelium		for a long time	diu
be	sum (irreg.)		forest	silva
beat	supero (1)		form a plan	consilium capio (3½)
beautiful	pulcher		forum	forum
because	quod		four	quattuor
big	magnus		freedman	libertus
book	liber		friend	amicus
boy	puer		frighten	terreo (2)
bravely	fortiter		from	a/ab + abl.
bright	clarus			
build	aedifico (1)		garden	hortus
but	sed		girl	puella
			give	do (1)
call	voco (1)		god	deus
capture	capio (3½)		goddess	dea
carry	porto (1)		go in	intro (1)
choose	lego (3)		gold	aurum
clear	clarus		good	bonus
come	venio (4)		great	magnus
comrade	socius		greatly	magnopere
country	patria		Greece	Graecia
crowd	turba		Greek	Graecus
			ground	terra
danger	periculum			
daughter	filia		handsome	pulcher
decide	constituo (3)		happy	laetus
deep	altus		have	habeo (2)

hear	audio (4)	nine	novem
		not	non
help	auxilium	now	iam
her (own)	suus		
here	hic	often	saepe
high	altus	on	in + abl.
his (own)	suus	one	unus
hold	teneo (2)	one day	olim
holy	sacer	order	iubeo (2)
homeland	patria	our	noster
horse	equus	out of	e/ex + abl.
house	villa	overcome	supero (1)
however	tamen		
hurry	festino (1)	place	locus
husband	maritus	plan	consilium
		play	ludo (3)
I	ego	poet	poeta
immediately	statim	praise	laudo (1)
in	in + abl.	prepare	paro (1)
inhabitant	incola	present, be	adsum (irreg.)
in this way	sic	prisoner	captivus
island	insula	put	pono (3)
kill	neco (1)	queen	regina
		(question)	-ne
land	terra		
laugh	rideo (2)	read	lego (3)
lead	duco (3)	receive	accipio (3½)
letter	epistula	remain	maneo (2)
like	amo (1)	reply	respondeo (2)
listen/listen to	audio (4)	road	via
little	parvus	Roman	Romanus
live	habito (1)	Rome	Roma
look at	specto (1)	rule	rego (3)
love	amo (1)	run	curro (3)
maidservant	ancilla	sacred	sacer
make	facio (3½)	safe	tutus
man	vir	sail	navigo (1)
many	multus	sailor	nauta
market place	forum	savage	saevus
master	dominus	say	dico (3)
meal	cena	see	video (2)
messenger	nuntius	send	mitto (3)
mine	meus	seven	septem
mistress	domina	shield	scutum
money	pecunia	shout	clamo (1)
move	moveo (2)	show	ostendo (3)
much	multus	sing	canto (1)
my	meus	six	sex
		sky	caelum
near	prope + acc.	slave	servus
never	numquam	slave-girl	ancilla
next	deinde	sleep	dormio (4)

small	parvus
son	filius
soon	mox
spear	hasta
stand	sto (1)
stay	maneo (2)
street	via
strong	validus
suddenly	subito
sword	gladius
take	capio (3½)
teacher	magister
temple	templum
ten	decem
their (own)	suus
then	deinde
there	ibi
therefore	igitur; itaque
three	tres
through	per + acc.
throw	iacio (3½)
thus	sic
tired	fessus
to	ad + acc.
towards	ad + acc.
town	oppidum
Trojan	Troianus
Troy	Troia
two	duo
unhappy	miser
villa	villa

walk	ambulo
wall	murus
want	cupio (3½)
war	bellum
warn	moneo (2)
watch	specto (1)
water	aqua
wave	unda
way	via
we	nos
well	bene
well known	notus
what?	quid?
when	ubi
where?	ubi?
who?	quis?
why?	cur?
wicked	malus
wind	ventus
wine	vinum
with	cum + abl.
wood	silva
woman	femina
word	verbum
work	laboro (1)
wretched	miser
write	scribo (3)
you (sg)	tu
you (pl)	vos
your (sg)	tuus
your (pl)	vester

List 6: Latin-English Quick Checklist

sg = singular pl = plural irreg. = irregular perf. = perfect imperf. = imperfect abl= ablative acc = accusative

a/ab + abl.	away from	ded-	(perf. of *do*)
abera-	(imperf. of *absum*)	deinde	then, next
adera-	(imperf. of *adsum*)	deleo (2)	I destroy
adfu-	(perf. of *adsum*)	deus	god
absum (irreg.)	I am away	dico (3)	I say
accep-	(perf. of *accipio*)	discedo (3)	I depart
accipio (3½)	I receive	diu	for a long time
ad + acc.	to, towards	dix-	(perf. of *dico*)
adsum (irreg.)	I am present	do (1)	I give
aedifico (1)	I build	domina	mistress
afu-	(perf. of *absum*)	dominus	master
ager	field	dormio (4)	I sleep
agricola	farmer	duco (3)	I lead
altus	high, deep	duo	two
ambulo (1)	I walk	dux-	(perf. of *duco*)
amicus	friend		
amo (1)	I like, love	e/ex + abl.	out of
ancilla	maidservant, slave-girl	ego	I
aqua	water	epistula	letter
audio (4)	I hear, listen to	equus	horse
aurum	gold	era-	(imperf. of *sum*)
auxilium	help	et	and
		etiam	also, even
bellum	war		
bene	well	facio (3½)	I do, make
bibo (3)	I drink	fec-	(perf. of *facio*)
bonus	good	femina	woman
		fessus	tired
caelum	sky	festino (1)	I hurry
canto (1)	I sing	filia	daughter
capio (3½)	I take, capture	filius	son
captivus	prisoner	fortiter	bravely
cena	dinner, meal	forum	forum, market place
cep-	(perf. of *capio*)	fu-	(perf. of *sum*)
cibus	food		
clamo (1)	I shout	gladius	sword
clarus	famous, bright, clear	Graecia	Greece
consilium	plan	Graecus	Greek
constituo (3)	decide		
consumo (3)	I eat	habeo (2)	I have
contra + acc.	against	habito (1)	I live
cucurr-	(perf. of *curro*)	hasta	spear
cum + abl.	with	hic	here
cupio (3½)	I want	hortus	garden
cur?	why?		
curro (3)	I run	iacio (3½)	I throw
		iam	now, already
de + abl.	down from, about	ibi	there
dea	goddess	iec-	(perf. of *iacio*)
decem	ten	igitur	therefore

in + abl	in, on	oppugno (1)	I attack
in + acc	into, onto	ostendo (3)	I show
incola	inhabitant		
insula	island	paro (1)	I prepare
intro (1)	I enter, go in	parvus	small, little
ira	anger	patria	homeland, country
iratus	angry	pecunia	money
itaque	and so, therefore	per + acc.	through, along
iterum	again	periculum	danger
iubeo (2)	I order	poeta	poet
iuss-	(perf. of *iubeo*)	pono (3)	I put
		porto (1)	I carry
laboro (1)	I work	posu-	(perf. of *pono*)
laetus	happy	proelium	battle
laudo (1)	I praise	prope + acc.	near
lego (3)	I read, choose	puella	girl
liber	book	puer	boy
libertus	freedman, ex-slave	pugno (1)	I fight
locus	place	pulcher	beautiful, handsome
ludo (3)	I play		
lus-	(perf. of *ludo*)	quattuor	four
		quid?	what?
magister	teacher	quinque	five
magnopere	greatly, especially	quis?	who?
magnus	big, great	quod	because
malus	bad, evil, wicked		
maneo (2)	I stay, remain	regina	queen
mans-	(perf. of *maneo*)	rego (3)	I rule
maritus	husband	respondeo (2)	I answer, reply
meus	my, mine	rex-	(perf. of *rego*)
mis-	(perf. of *mitto*)	rideo (2)	I laugh
miser	wretched, unhappy		
mitto (3)	I send	ris-	(perf. of *rideo*)
moneo (2)	I warn	rogo (1)	I ask, ask for
moveo (2)	I move	Roma	Rome
mox	soon	Romanus	Roman
multus	much, many		
murus	wall	sacer	holy, sacred
		saepe	often
nauta	sailor	saevus	savage
navigo (1)	I sail	sagitta	arrow
-ne?	(indicates a question)	scribo (3)	I write
neco (1)	I kill	scrips-	(perf. of *scribo*)
non	not	scutum	shield
nos	we	sed	but
noster	our	semper	always
notus	well known	septem	seven
novem	nine	servus	slave
numquam	never	sex	six
nuntius	messenger	sic	thus, in this way
		silva	wood, forest
octo	eight	socius	ally, comrade
olim	one day	specto (1)	I look at, watch
oppidum	town	statim	immediate

stet-	(perf. of *sto*)	tutus	safe
sto (1)	I stand	tuus	your (sg)
subito	suddenly		
sum (irreg.)	I am	ubi	when
supero (1)	I overcome, beat	ubi?	where?
suus	his/her/their own	unda	wave
		unus	one
tamen	however		
tandem	finally, at last	validus	strong
templum	temple	venio (4)	I come
teneo (2)	I hold	ventus	wind
terra	land, ground	verbum	word
terreo (2)	I frighten	vester	your (pl)
timeo (2)	I fear	via	road, street, way
trans + acc.	across	video (2)	I see
tres	three	villa	villa, house
Troia	Troy	vinum	wine
Troianus	Trojan	vir	man
tu	you (sg)	voco (1)	I call
turba	crowd	vos	you (pl)

Printed in Great Britain
by Amazon

85406616R00086